Proportional Representation Applied To Party Government

THOMAS RAMSDEN ASHWORTH

1901

TABLE OF CONTENTS

PREFACE

The subject of electoral reform has been brought into prominence in Australia by a clause in the Commonwealth Bill which provides that the Federal Senate shall consist of six senators from each State, directly chosen by the people, voting as one electorate. The problem thus presented has been keenly discussed. On the one hand we have the advocates of the Block Vote asserting that the party in a majority is entitled to return all six senators; and on the other, a small band of ardent reformers pressing the claims of the Hare system, which would allow the people in each State to group themselves into six sections, each returning one senator. The claim that every section of the people is entitled to representation appears at first sight so just that it seems intolerable that a method should have been used all these years which excludes the minority in each electorate from any share of representation; and, of course, the injustice becomes more evident when the electorate returns several members. But in view of the adage that it is the excellence of old institutions which preserves them, it is surely a rash conclusion that the present method of election has no compensating merit. We believe there is such a merit—namely, that the present method of election has developed the party system. Once this truth is grasped, it is quite evident that the Hare system would be absolutely destructive to party government, since each electorate would be contested, not by two organized parties, but by several groups. For it is precisely this splitting into groups which is causing such anxiety among thoughtful observers as to the future of representative institutions; Mr. Lecky has attributed to it, in his "Democracy and Liberty," the decline in the parliamentary system which has accompanied the progress of democracy all over the world. The object

5

of this book is to suggest a reform, which possesses the advantages of both methods and the disadvantages of neither; which will still ensure that each electorate is contested by the two main parties, but will allow its just share of representation to each; and which will, by discouraging the formation of minor groups, provide a remedy for the evil instead of aggravating it.
T.R.A.
H.P.C.A.
325 COLLINS STREET, MELBOURNE.
PROPORTIONAL REPRESENTATION APPLIED TO PARTY GOVERNMENT.

THE TRUE PRINCIPLES OF POLITICAL REPRESENTATION

Old establishments, like the British Constitution, said Edmund Burke, "are not often constructed after any theory; theories are rather drawn from them." In setting out on an endeavour to understand the principles underlying political representation, the saying expresses exactly the course which should be followed. The inquiry is the more necessary as, although representation more than anything else in the domain of government distinguishes the modern from the ancient world, the ideas which prevail as to the part it has played, is playing, and is destined to play on the world's stage are not merely hazy, but extremely inaccurate. The intimate connection of representation with the progress which has followed its introduction is so little recognized that the most advanced democracies are now willing to listen to any proposal to return to direct government. In spite of the fact that the nineteenth century has witnessed the triumph of the historical method in most fields of social inquiry, the dangers of a priori speculation on political institutions are as much in evidence as when Burke wrote.

If we would understand, then, the meaning of representative institutions, it is in the gradual development of the "mother of parliaments" that we must seek for the most reliable information. We must be careful, however, to leave out of sight those features of the growth of the British Constitution which are merely the expression of transitory social conditions, and to confine our attention to the landmarks which bear directly on the inquiry. The subject is best divided into two stages; the first characterized by the origin of representation; and the second by the division into parties, and the creation of cabinet government.

The First Stage of Representation.—Rightly to understand the conditions

7

which led to the introduction and development of the representative principle, we must look back to the period immediately following the signing of the Great Charter by the tyrant King John.

The Charter reaffirmed the ancient principle that free Englishmen should not be taxed without their consent, and representation was the natural outcome of that provision. A brief glance at the social conditions of the time is necessary to understand why this was so. First, it must be remembered that the true political unit of ancient times was the city or local community. England at that time was a collection of local communities, having more or less a corporate life. Then, again, there were the three estates of the realm—the clergy, the lords, and the commons—who were accustomed to confer with the King on public affairs. The stage which marks the birth of representation was when these different estates and communities were asked to tax themselves to relieve the necessities of the King. It was obviously impossible that the consent of every freeman should be obtained, hence the duty had to be deputed to agents. Now, the idea of agency was not unknown in the ancient world, but that agents should have power to bind those for whom they acted was something entirely new. It was necessary, however, that they should have this power, and it suited the King's convenience that they should exercise it. Already, in the earliest writ of which we have knowledge, summoning each shire to send two good and discreet knights, it was provided that they should be chosen in the stead of each and all. This happened in 1254, and in the following year the clergy were also summoned for the same purpose of granting aid to the King. In the meantime the merchants and trade guilds in the cities were growing rich. The King cast longing eyes on their possessions, and wished to tax them. So we find that in 1264 Simon de Montfort, Earl of Leicester, issued the celebrated writ summoning each of the cities and boroughs to send two of its more discreet and worthy citizens and burgesses. This is sometimes regarded as the beginning of the House of Commons, but it was really not until the fourteenth century that these several assemblies, each of which up till then taxed itself separately and legislated in its own sphere, coalesced into the present Houses. First the lower clergy fell out, and, with the knights, citizens, and burgesses, were merged into the House of Commons; and the higher prelates with the earls and barons formed the House of Lords.

This, then, is the first stage of representation. What was the nature of this new force which had come into the world and was destined to so profoundly affect the whole course of human affairs? One result of immense importance is apparent at a glance. It solved a problem which had baffled the ancients—that of the nationalization of local communities on a free basis. But it is generally assumed that the only difficulty overcome was that of size; that the representative assembly is a mere substitute for the larger assembly of the whole nation. Starting with this assumption, it is claimed that the representative assembly should be a mirror of the people on a small scale, and the more faithfully it reflects their faults as well as their virtues, their ignorance as well as their intelligence, the more truly representative it is said to be. It is even asserted that with the modern facilities for taking a poll, representative government might be dispensed with and the people allowed to govern themselves. Democracy, we are assured, means that every man should exercise an equality of political power. Now, if this conception is correct, we should at once insist that every law should be submitted to a direct referendum of the people; that legislators should be mere agents for drawing up laws; and that the executive should be directly responsible to and elected by the people. But if representation is not a mere substitute for the direct action of the people this idea as to the true line of democratic progress falls to the ground. The whole question, therefore, hinges on what representation is and what are the principles underlying it.

Looking back to the history of its introduction, we have seen that it was only in proportion as the deputies of the local communities were not regarded as delegates or agents that they became representatives. Professor E. Jenks has written an interesting article in the Contemporary Review for December, 1898, in which he advances the theory that representation is a union of the ideas of agency, borrowed from the Roman law, and of vicarious liability from barbaric sources. As to the latter he points out that in Anglo-Saxon times the only way for the King to control the free local communities was to exact hostages till crimes were punished or fines paid. In England, where these ideas were combined, constitutional monarchy was firmly established; but in France, Germany, etc, in whose medieval parliaments the idea of agency prevailed, and where in consequence the parliamentary idea was weak, absolute monarchy held its ground. When Edward I. desired for purposes of his own to emphasize the unlimited liability of political representatives, and insisted that they should have "full and sufficient power to do what of common council shall be ordained," he probably never realized that a body having power to bind the shires and towns was a formidable institution, or that the trembling hostages would become in time haughty plenipotentiaries. But whatever may have been the social conditions which gave rise to the idea, it is certain that it was the power of binding those to whom they owed their selection which enabled the representatives to resist the encroachments of the monarchy on the liberties of the people. At first they were not legislators, but merely sought to uphold the ancient laws. They presented petitions to redress their grievances; but in time these petitions became demands; and they refused to grant the King's subsidies till the demands were complied with. It was, therefore, this first stage of representation which enabled the people to start that long struggle against the power of the King and nobles which has ended in complete self-government; nay, more, it was necessary that they should pass through this first stage before they could learn to govern themselves. Yet we have seen that if we apply the modern ideas on representation the start could never have been made. In what respects, then, did these early representative institutions differ from the modern conception as a reproduction of the people on a small scale? One obvious difference at once suggests itself. The representatives were not average members of the communities; they were the most influential; they were selected because of their special fitness for the work to be done; they were leaders of the people, not followers; they did not take inspiration from the people, but brought it to them; and having selected these men the people deferred to their judgment to act for them and protect their interests. Here, then, we arrive at the first principle involved in representation, which is leadership.

But there is another and still more important difference between a representative assembly and a primary assembly of the people. It is this: that a representative cannot be a violent partisan of a small section of his constituents; he must be in general favour with all sections. Therefore a representative assembly is composed of moderate men, representing a compromise of the views of their individual supporters. Moreover, the representatives appeal to the people to sink their minor differences for the general welfare. This feature is very prominent in the early parliaments. The local communities were arrayed as a united people against the aggression of the monarchy. The principle which is here apparent is that of organization. In the first stage of English parliamentary history we may say at once that these two principles—organization and leadership—were most conspicuous. The people, sinking all minor differences, formed one united party; and recognised that their struggle against the party of prerogative depended on the ability, influence, and integrity of their deputies.

The Second Stage of Representation.—There is no need to enter into that long struggle between the nation and the monarchy which followed. We pass on, then, to the time when the parliaments, having wrested a share of power, began to split up into parties. It was natural that when power became divided two parties should arise; one upholding the authority of the Parliament against the King; and the other favouring the divine right of Kings. The Puritans and Cavaliers in the troublous times of Charles I. were the earliest signs of this tendency. The Long Parliament, which met in 1640, was divided on these lines; the misdemeanors of the King brought on civil war; the parliamentary troops defeated the royal troops after a bloody struggle; and the King was brought to execution. The succeeding events were full of instruction. The Parliament attempted to govern the nation—or, rather, we should say the House of Commons did, for the House of

Lords was abolished. But it proved quite unfit for the purpose. It was thoroughly disorganized, and rent by violent factions. The anarchy which ensued was ended by a military despot, Oliver Cromwell, who entered the House of Commons in 1653 with his soldiers. The Speaker was pulled from his chair; the members were driven from the House; and Cromwell was proclaimed dictator. It is strange, indeed, that the lesson which is to be drawn from this event, and which has been repeated in France time after time since the Revolution, has not yet been learned: the only escape from continued political anarchy is despotism. But the weakness of despotism is that it ends with the life of the despot. Cromwell's son was forced to abdicate, and the monarchy was restored. The same division of parties in the Parliament continued, and they began to take the names of Whigs and Tories. Towards the end of the seventeenth century, the dissensions of these two factions again threatened to make government impossible. In administration the evil was felt most; the union of ministers of both parties was proving unworkable. So fickle did legislation become that no one could say one day what the House would do the next. It was at this crisis, and about the year 1693, that William III., who cared more for a strong administration than for political differences, created what is known as cabinet government, and, as Professor Gardiner says, "refounded the government of England on a new basis." Recognizing that power should not be separated from responsibility, he affirmed the principle that the ministers of state should be selected from the party which had a majority in the House of Commons. But the time was not yet ripe for the complete application of this principle. Early in the eighteenth century Sir Robert Walpole set the example of resigning when he no longer possessed the confidence of a majority of the House of Commons; but in the latter half of the century the great Earl of Chatham introduced again the practice of selecting ministers irrespective of party. Despite the fact that he was supported by the personal influence of George III., the attempt failed. A succession of weak ministries followed; and out of the confusion the modern division of Liberals and Conservatives emerged. Thus it was not until the beginning of the present century that the doctrines of the solidarity of the Cabinet and its complete dependence on a majority of the House of Commons were thoroughly developed in their present form. England, now grown into the United Kingdom, had at last, after six centuries of strife, won her national independence, and for one brief century has enjoyed a full measure of self-government.

Comparison of the Two Stages.—How do the conditions presented by the nineteenth century differ from those of the fourteenth? And how is the problem of representation affected? We have seen that the great forces which animated the nation in the fourteenth century were organization and leadership. Have these forces ceased to operate? Assuredly not. In the fourteenth century we had a united people organized under its chosen leaders against the encroachments of the King and nobility on its national liberty. In the nineteenth century the people have won their political independence, but the struggle is now carried on between two great organized parties. The principle of leadership is still as strong as ever. The careers of Pitt, Peel, Palmerston, Beaconsfield, and Gladstone attest that fact. The one great difference, then, between the fourteenth and the nineteenth centuries is that instead of one party there are two. The problem of representation in the fourteenth century was to keep the people together in one united party, and to allow them to select their most popular leaders. Surely the problem is different in the nineteenth century. The requirements now are to organize the people into two great parties, and to allow each party separately to elect its most popular leaders. And yet we are still using the same method of election as our forefathers used six centuries ago. Although the conditions have entirely changed, we have not adapted the electoral machinery to the change. The system of single-membered electorates was rational in the fourteenth century, because there was only one party. Is it not on the face of it absurd to-day, when there are two parties?

The Meaning of Party Government.—Why should there be two parties instead of one in order that the people should be able to govern themselves? To answer this question we must start at the beginning, and consider what is the problem of popular government. The best definition is that it is to promote the general welfare—to reconcile or average the real interests of all sections of the community. Now, if the people could all agree what is best in the interests of all, unity of action might certainly be obtained; but even then the problem would not be solved, for the people are not infallible. The greater part of the problem consists in finding out what is best in the interests of all, and no amount of mere abstract speculation can solve this part. So diverse and so complex are the interests to be reconciled, so interwoven and interdependent one with another, that the problem of securing a just balance is incapable of solution by anything short of omniscience. But in any case the people cannot be always got to agree to one course of action. Therefore the people cannot govern themselves as one united party. The only workable basis is, then, the rule of the majority, and the problem of popular government is how to ensure that the majority shall rule in the interests of all.

Party government provides the best known means of solving this problem. The only way of finding out what is best for the whole people is by the incessant action and interaction of two great organized parties under their chosen leaders; each putting forth its energies to prove its fitness to hold the reins of government; each anxious to expose the defects of the other. This healthy emulation as to what is best for all, with the people to judge, is the real secret of free government. The two parties are virtually struggling as to which shall be king. Each is striving to gain the support of a majority of the people; and the grounds on which it appeals for support are that the measures it proposes are the best for the country, and that the men it puts forward are the best men for passing those measures into law and carrying on the administration of the country. This constant agitation, and this mutual competition to devise new measures, and to bring forward new men, prevent stagnation. Both sides of every leading public question of the day are presented in the rival party policies, and the people are invited to decide between them. The forces on which the parties rely to move the people are enthusiasm for measures and enthusiasm for men—party and personality, or, in other words, organization and leadership. It is in opposing these forces to counteract the selfish and anti-social passions that party government acquires its virtue. By appealing to their higher nature it induces the people to subordinate their class prejudices to the general welfare, and by setting before them definite moral ideals, and appealing to them by the force of personality, it raises the character of public opinion, and moulds individual and national character to an extent that is seldom appreciated. Here, then, is the key of human progress. Direct democracies may hold together so long as there are external enemies to induce the people to sink their differences in the common interest, or so long as there is a slave caste to do the menial work, as in the ancient democracies; but representative democracy offers the only hope of welding together a free people into a united whole. The unrestrained rule of the majority under direct democracy must degenerate into the tyranny of the majority. Instead of the equality of political power which it promises, the minority is deprived of all power. Representative democracy, on the other hand, deprives the people of the personal exercise of political power, in order to save them from the free play of their self-assertive passions, but still leaves to every man an equality of influence in deciding the direction of progress. Thus every man is induced to express his opinion as to the direction of progress; and the party policy is the resultant direction of progress of all the party electors, and therefore represents their organized opinion. Now, bear in mind that the true direction of progress is not known, and can only be found out by constant experiment directed by the most far-seeing and capable minds. It is the means of carrying on this experiment which party government provides. The party representing the organized opinion of the majority has, rightly, complete control of the direction of progress so long as it remains in a majority. But, although deliberation is the work of many, execution is the work of one. Hence the creation of a small committee of the party in power—the cabinet—associated with the leader of the party, who becomes for the time being the Prime Minister, the cabinet ministers being jointly responsible for the control of administration and the initiation of measures for the public good. But an organized minority is quite as essential to progress as an organized majority—not merely to oppose, but to criticise and expose the errors of the party in power, and to supplant it when it ceases to possess the confidence of the country. Hence progress under party government may be compared to a zigzag line, in which the changes in direction correspond to changes in ministry. By this mutual action and alternation of parties every vote cast has, in the long run, an equal influence in guiding progress. The only justification for majority rule sanctioned by free government is that when two parties differ as to what is best for the whole people the majority shall prevail, and party government tends to realize this condition. But direct government by the people offers no check whatever on the power of the majority, which is as absolute as that of the Czar of Russia. As Calhoun, the American statesman, writes in his "Disquisition on Government," "the principle by which constitutional governments are upheld, is compromise, that of absolute governments is force!" Now, the significance of party government as a guarantee of free government lies in this: that party policies represent a compromise of what every section composing each party supposes to be the interests of the whole people; and the parties are engaged in fighting out a compromise of the real interests of every section of the people.

Lest it be thought that in this panegyric on party government we have been indulging in a wild flight into the region of speculative politics, we hasten to add that the ideal condition we have pictured has never been reached. The British Parliament has perhaps most nearly approached it, but already shows signs of retrogression. America and the Australian colonies are drifting further away from it. Already political philosophers are shaking their heads and predicting the failure of popular government. The cry everywhere is for a stronger executive. Party organization is breaking down; small factions actuated by self-interest hold the balance of power between the main parties, and render government unstable and capricious. The main parties themselves tend to degenerate into factions. Personality is declining—the demand is for followers, not leaders. Compromise is supplanted by log-rolling and lobbying. And, to crown all, the rumbling of class strife grows ominously louder. The danger is that these tendencies may be allowed to go too far before reform is attempted—that the confidence between classes may be destroyed.

Organization and Leadership.—We have shown that the two great principles underlying representation are organization and leadership. Now, after all, there is nothing very profound in this conclusion. Is there a single department of concerted human action in which these same principles are not apparent? What would be thought of an army without discipline and without generals; or of a musical production in which every performer played his own tune? Even in the region of sport, can a cricket or a football team dispense with its captain and its places? And yet many people imagine that a disorganized collection of delegates of various sections can rule a nation? Such an assembly would be as much a mob as any primary assembly of the people, and would in no sense be a representative assembly. The fact is that the growing intensity of the evils which beset representative institutions throughout the civilized world to-day is due to imperfect expression of these two principles. Representative assemblies are not properly organized into two coherent parties, nor is each party allowed free play to select its most popular leaders. What is the remedy?

A Change in Electoral Machinery the Key to Reform.—The great mistake made by all writers on electoral reform is that they have failed to recognize that the character of public opinion depends upon the way it is expressed. If the electoral machinery be adapted to give effect to those principles of organization and leadership which lie at the root of representation, then the character of public opinion will be improved. Representation, in fact, is not only a means of expressing public opinion, but also of guiding, informing, educating, and organizing it. Therefore, the method of election is an all-important factor.

The first and greatest necessity is to counteract the tendency of the people to split up into factions. It may seem a startling conclusion that this is a mere matter of electoral machinery, but it is nevertheless quite true. It must be remembered that we are dealing with human beings and not with insentient figures. If the method of election allows representation to two sections only, the people will group themselves into two sections. But if it allows representation to a large number of sections, then the people will group themselves into as many sections as are allowed. Now, party government offers every hope of preventing two sections degenerating into factions, but with a number of sections there is absolutely none.

Here, then, we see the one great merit of the present system of election, which explains why it has persisted so long, with all its faults. It is that it tends to confine representation to the two main parties, since each electorate is generally contested by them; but in so far as it does not completely effect that object and allows representation to independent factions it is defective. Moreover, the merit we have indicated is purchased at too high a price. It is these defects which are causing the degradation of representative institutions throughout the world to-day.

It is obviously impossible to give a just share of representation to two parties and allow each party to elect its most popular leaders, in an electorate which returns only a single representative. Hence the first necessity for reform is to enlarge electorates, so that each may return several representatives. Now, the requirements for giving effect to the principles of organization and leadership in such an electorate are:—

1. Proportional representation to the two main parties—Ministerial and

Opposition, the majority and the minority.

2. The election by each party of its most popular candidates—i.e., those most in general favour with all sections of the party.

This is the problem of representation as it presents itself to us. Leaving a detailed account of the means by which it is proposed to give effect to these great desiderata to a later chapter, let us indicate briefly where they strike at the root of the evils of the present system.

Enlarged Electorates.—With enlarged electorates the minority will not be excluded. Each party will secure its just share of representation. When both parties are represented in each electorate the interests of the electorate will not be bargained for as the price of support. Members will cease to be mere local delegates.

Proportional Representation to the Two Main Parties.—Representation must be absolutely confined to the two main parties, and each party must be allowed its just share. Every candidate should be required to nominate either as a Ministerialist or Oppositionist, and each party should be allotted a number of representatives proportional to the total amount of support received. If democracy means that every man's opinion, as expressed by his vote, is to have the same weight, it follows that the parties should be represented in the Legislature in the same proportion as among the people, otherwise it is ridiculous to talk of the rule of the majority. The present system sometimes results in minority rule and sometimes in minority extermination; it is difficult to say which alternative is the worse.

Election of its Most Popular Candidates by each Party.—It would be little use to confine representation to the two main parties if the parties were allowed to split up into factions. The only way to prevent this is to provide such electoral machinery as will ensure the return of the candidates most in general favour with all sections, and will exclude the favourites of sections within the party. This distinction is vital. The general favourite is a representative; the favourite of a faction is a delegate. A representative is not only independent of any one section, but if he does favour a faction he will sink in general favour. He therefore represents a compromise of the demands of all sections. But a delegate is the mouthpiece of a faction—a follower, not a leader of the people.

No section will be disfranchised by this proposal, for the true function of all minor sections is to influence the policies of the two main parties. Thus every section will be proportionally represented in one or the other policy and by all the party candidates. Not only will each party be proportionally represented but all the sections which compose each party will be proportionally represented in its policy. This is the only true meaning of proportional representation.

THE SO-CALLED REPRESENTATIVE PRINCIPLE

All schemes of electoral reform hitherto proposed under the name of proportional representation are based on the so-called "representative principle"—viz., that every section of the people is entitled to separate representation in proportion to its numbers. The ideal varies somewhat, but the usual conception, is that if each member represents a different section or interest the assembly will represent all sections or all interests. Now this is simply an attempt to return to what we have described as the first stage of representation, but without the fear of the monarchy to keep the sections together. For a deliberative body or a king's council it might be suitable, but for an assembly charged with the complete control of government in the interests of all it is utterly impracticable. Each representative must represent all interests; he must be elected on a definite policy as to what is best for all the people. If he is sent in as the agent of one interest or one section of the people, he ceases to be a representative and becomes a delegate. All these schemes are therefore not proportional representation at all, but proportional delegation.

We have shown that representation means the organization of public opinion into two definite lines of policy, and that this is the only way to prevent political anarchy. But the proportionalists (as they like to call themselves) say that it means representing men and the opinions they hold in proportion to their numbers. The fundamental error is that they neglect the all-important factor of human nature. They look on public opinion as something having an independent existence apart from the questions about which it is expressed and from the means of expressing it; and they fail to recognize that the character of public opinion depends on the manner in which it is expressed and organized. It is but a natural consequence that they also conceive the number of sections of opinion awaiting representation as pre-existing and independent of the electoral machinery.

In short, they reduce the whole problem to a nice little exercise in mathematics, requiring only for its clear exposition some columns of figures and a few coloured diagrams to represent the different shades of public opinion. No better example of the dangers of a priori speculation could be adduced than this chimerical idea of the proportionalists that public opinion is something to be divided into fractions like a mathematical quantity, unless it be, perhaps, the conclusion that if you gather together delegates representing these fractions you will have an assembly representing the sum total of public opinion.

The issue is quite clear. Are we to have two parties aiming at the control of administration and appealing to all sections for support, or the separate delegation of a number of sections? In the one case we will have parties based on national policies, and in the other case we will have a number of factions, each wanting something different and determined to block progress till it gets it. Remember that it is a mere matter of electoral machinery which will determine the choice. It is true that at present we do not have two very coherent parties, but that is the fault of the present electoral system.

It would seem that there can be but one answer to this question, and yet the "representative principle" shows such wonderful vitality that it is worth while considering the arguments on which it is based, and the various stages through which the idea has passed.

Mr. Hare's Scheme.—The "representative principle" was first propounded in England in 1857 by Mr. Thomas Hare. He proposed that the United Kingdom should be constituted one huge electorate for the return of the 654 members of the House of Commons. The people were to group themselves into 654 voluntary unanimous sections, each returning one member, and each gathered from every corner of the kingdom. We propose to consider here not the scheme itself but only the principle on which it was founded. Mr. Hare rightly conceived that the great evil of the present system is the exclusion of the minority in each electorate, but he altogether failed to appreciate that the excluded minority nearly always represented one of the two main parties. He could not see, in fact, that to divide each electorate into majority and minority is to divide the whole country into majority and minority, nor that the injustice is tolerated because it is usually as bad for one party as the other. Instead, therefore, of proposing to do justice to both the majority and the minority in each electorate, he proposed to allow representation to as many minorities as possible. To him, the rule of the majority was the rule of a majority of interests; this he called the constitutional majority, as opposed to the "mere rule of numbers." Now, at the time Mr. Hare wrote party government was rather weak in England. He quotes with approval a statement of Mr. Sidney Herbert, M.P., that the

House was divided into many parties, or rather no party, because the country was divided into many parties or no party, and that the division into two parties would never be restored again. It is amusing, in view of after events, to find Mr. Hare asking what would be the result of any contrivance to re-establish party. Assuming that party representation was dead, Mr. Hare proposed to substitute personal representation. It is positively ludicrous at this interval of time to note how the electors were expected to group themselves. They were to take personal merit as the basis of representation; every vote cast was to be a spontaneous tribute to the qualities and attainments of the person for whom it was given. And in order, presumably, that they should choose good men in preference to corrupt men, the polling-day was to be set apart as a sacred holiday, and church services were to be held to solemnize the public act and seek for the Divine blessing!

The maintenance of a responsible ministry in such a House presented no difficulty to Mr. Hare. The electors were to indicate whom they considered the most illustrious statesmen, and no one would dare to question their decision!

It seems strange now that this scheme should have received serious consideration. Mr. Hare was so much under the spell of the apparent justice of the underlying principle that he was blind to its results. But it was soon perceived that the electors would not group themselves as Mr. Hare supposed; that the personal ideal of every class of electors would be simply men of their own class. It was further pointed out that cranks and faddists and every organization founded on questions of the remotest interest would combine to secure representation. Mr. Disraeli declared it to be "opposed to every sound principle, its direct effect being to create a stagnant representation ... an admirable scheme for bringing crotchety men into the House." Mr. Shaw-Lefevre condemned it as "a vicious principle based upon a theory of classes," and Mr. Gladstone said that it regarded electors "not as rational and thinking beings, but merely as the equivalents of one another." Walter Bagehot, in his standard work on the "English Constitution," opposes the principle of voluntary constituencies, because it would promote a constituency-making trade. "But upon the plan suggested," he writes, "the House would be made up of party politicians selected by a party committee, chained to that committee, and pledged to party violence, and of characteristic, and therefore unmoderate, representatives for every 'ism' in all England. Instead of a deliberate assembly of moderate and judicious men, we should have a various compound of all sorts of violence. I may seem to be drawing a caricature, but I have not reached the worst. Bad as these members would be if they were left to themselves—if in a free Parliament they were confronted with the perils of government, close responsibility might improve them, and make them tolerable. But they would not be left to themselves. A voluntary constituency will nearly always be a despotic constituency."

The practical difficulties in the application of Mr. Hare's scheme are almost insuperable, but it is not worth while pursuing the subject, since it is now admitted by recent advocates that the faddist argument is fatal. This is an admission that Mr. Hare completely neglected the factor of human nature. Professor Nanson writes:—"Hare proposed that there should be only one electorate, consisting of the whole State. It is unfortunate that this proposal was made. There can be no doubt that it has retarded the progress of true electoral reform for at least a generation ... it would inevitably lead to the election of a certain number of faddists."

John Stuart Mill.—The great vogue which the Hare system has obtained is to be traced more to the influence of John Stuart Mill than to that of anyone else. Mill was captivated by the apparent justice of the proposal, and devoted a chapter of his "Representative Government" to it, wherein he declared:—"Mr. Hare's scheme has the almost unparalleled merit of carrying out a great principle of government in a manner approaching to ideal perfection, while it attains incidentally several other things of scarcely inferior importance." Believing in the absolute justice of the principle, Mill and Hare were certainly consistent in setting no limit to its application except the size of the assembly. Mill is emphatic on this point. "Real equality of representation," he asserted, "is not obtained unless any set of electors, amounting to average number of a constituency, wherever they happen to reside, have the power of combining with one another to return a representative." Now, the recent disciples of Mr. Hare are never tired of claiming the support of Mill, although they have thrown this definition to the winds. But they are guilty of far more than that, for in another chapter of Mill's book we find that his conception of a representative assembly elected by the Hare system is a purely deliberative body. He expressly declares it to be radically unfit for legislation, which he proposes to hand over to a commission appointed by the Crown. The value of his testimony is very much discounted by this fact.

Sir John Lubbock.[1]—We have asserted that the proportional principle should be applied to two parties only—the majority and the minority, and that every section can then be represented. Mill and Hare thought that no limit should be set except the size of the assembly. All the recent advocates of the system take up an intermediate position. Appreciating the serious objections against allowing independent representation to a large number of small sections, Sir John Lubbock, president of the English Proportional Representation Society, proposes to constitute electorates returning only three to five members each, thus confining representation to only three to five sections in each electorate, and sacrificing to a great extent accurate proportional representation. In his book on "Representation," he writes:—

"I have assumed that Parliament should be 'a mirror of the nation;' if the object were to secure unity of action rather than freedom of discussion, to form an executive body such as a Government, a Board of Directors, or a Vestry, the case would be quite different. It is, however, I presume, our wish that Parliament should be a deliberative assembly in which all parties should be fairly represented." But to make Parliament a deliberative body is to destroy its power to secure unity of action at all, and to render it useless as a working machine.

Miss Spence.—An active campaign has for some time been carried on for the adoption of the Hare system in Australia. Miss C.H. Spence, of South Australia, was the pioneer reformer, and has laboured in the cause by pen and voice for no less than forty years. Great credit is undoubtedly due to Miss Spence for the clear and simple manner in which she has expounded the system, and for the good work she has done in exposing the defects of the present methods. Not only has she lectured in all parts of Australia, but she has made visits to England, where she met Mr. Hare and Sir John Lubbock, and also to America. But we may admire Miss Spence's courage and devotion to principle without agreeing with her conclusions.

At a meeting held at River House, Chelsea, London, in 1894, Miss Spence submitted an analysis of 8,824 votes recorded at 50 public meetings in South Australia. The audiences were in each case asked to select six representatives out of twelve candidates. The result of a scrutiny of all the votes combined was that the following six "parties" secured one "representative" each—viz., Capital, Labour, Single Tax, Irish Catholic, Prohibition, and Women's Suffrage. Miss Spence frankly confesses that these "parties" are minorities, but holds that a majority can be formed by the union of minorities, and that party responsible government can still be carried on. Now, can any sensible man or woman imagine a working ministry formed by a union of any four of these "parties?" Capital would certainly be permanently opposed to Labour and to Single Tax, and as for the others, there is not a single principle in common. How, then, could a union be formed? The only possible way is by log-rolling; they must make a bargain to support one another's demands. Such a union could not possibly be stable, because the minority is free to offer a better bargain to any one of the "parties" to induce it to desert. Again, it may be called the rule of the majority, but what sort of a majority? Is it not plainly the rule of a majority in the interests of minorities? That is very different to the rule of the majority in the interests of all, which free government demands. The simple truth is that the "parties" are factions, and that the "representatives" are mere delegates of those factions.

But in practice the case would be far worse than we have assumed. There is not the slightest guarantee that the same six factions would be elected in each six-seat electorate. We might have an unlimited number of delegates of various religions, classes, races, localities, and political organizations on all kinds of single questions. An assembly formed on these lines could hardly be dignified with the name of a representative assembly.

Mr. G. Bradford, in his work on "The Lesson of Popular Government," displays a more intimate knowledge of human nature than any other recent writer. Of these schemes for the representation of minorities he says:—

As an illustration of the effect in popular government of looking to popular impulse for the initiation of measures, it may be observed that perhaps the worst of all expedients for remedying the defective working of a government by a legislature like ours, that which combines the evils of them all, is one which is urged by perfectly disinterested advocates of reform, and is known as proportional representation. If there is one principle at the base of popular government it is that the majority shall rule. If the largest of three or four fractions is to rule it ceases to be popular government, and becomes government by faction. If the tyranny of the majority is bad a tyranny of the minority is still worse. (Vol. i., p. 505.)

And the following picture could hardly be better drawn:—

If the basis of carrying on the government is to be the wishes of some millions of units, it is evident that they must to a greater or less extent agree in wishing for something. It is equally evident that they cannot all agree in wishing for the same thing at the same time, while if they, or any considerable number of groups, want different things at the same time, the result in so far is anarchy. Government is paralysed, and with the well-known excitability of humanity in groups men begin to confound the importance of the thing wanted with the importance of getting what they want. The clash of contending factions is apt to suggest the clash of arms. The first necessity, therefore, is the formation of large and coherent parties, not merely for the purpose of accomplishing what is desired by the majority of the people, but also for suppressing agitation and social disturbance on behalf of what may be called merely objects of passion or private interest with comparatively small groups, at least until those objects enlist the support of a large minority. (Vol. i., pp. 492, 493.)

Professor Nanson.—In Victoria the Hare system is championed by Mr. E.J. Nanson, Professor of Mathematics at Melbourne University. Professor Nanson approaches the subject entirely from a mathematical standpoint, and resolutely refuses to admit the factor of human nature into his calculations. Following Mr. Hare, he is a declared opponent of party government, and "would like to see it pushed further into the background." Moreover, he regards every step in the process as an end in itself. Thus the act of voting is one end, representation is another, and the rule of the majority a third. Leaving aside for the present, however, the elaborate mathematical devices which are proposed for attaining these supposed ends, let us take only the principles on which they are based. These are laid down as follows:——

(a) The rule of the majority.

(b) The fair representation of all parties in proportion to their strength.

(c) Perfect freedom to every elector to vote exactly as he pleases.

(d) The emancipation of the voters from the tyranny of the political "boss" or caucus.

(e) The full value of his vote to each voter without loss or waste.

The principles involved, we are assured, "must appeal to every democrat, to every Liberal, to every lover of true and just representation."

As to the first claim, we are willing to grant the rule of the majority, if the words are added "in the interests of minorities." The second could also be granted if by "all parties" were meant both parties, for there cannot be more than two parties in the true sense of the word. But Professor Nanson proposes such large electorates that any small section, from one-sixth to one-twelfth, can secure independent representation. Notwithstanding this, he claims that it is quite possible to give fair representation to the main parties and to small sections at the same time. In illustrating the system he avoids the issue as to the character of these sections by giving them a "scientific" nomenclature, such as Colour, Place, Pursuits, Qualities, andc. These abstractions are very misleading, as attention is diverted from the fact that they refer to voluntary groups of men united for some political purpose. The real question is, on what basis are these groups likely to be formed? When the element of human nature is taken into account it must be apparent that they will be formed for the propaganda of some sectional interest; some on a religious basis, others on a class basis, andc. Now, if we were to ask each candidate to declare his religion, we could easily take religions as the basis of representation and allow proportional representation to each religion; and similarly with classes, races, and so on. But we could only take one basis at a time, and the important deduction is that if we were to take religions as the basis of representation, the people would be induced to vote according to religion; if we were to take classes, according to class, and so on. Now, no one but the fanatic or the demagogue will claim that the majority is entitled to rule where religions only or classes only are represented. The questions then arise—What is the correct basis of representation? How should the people be induced to vote? And the answer is clearly that the people should be induced to vote on questions of general public policy, on the leading questions of the day which decide the party lines, and that, therefore, the policies of the two main parties should form the primary basis of proportional representation. But the Hare system, by taking individual candidates as the basis of representation, induces the elector to vote on any basis or on sectional lines. It promotes dissension instead of repressing it, and instead of encouraging all sections to express their opinion as to what is best for the general well-being, it encourages them to express their opinion as to what they imagine to be best for themselves. Public opinion expressed on these lines would be worse than useless. But Professor Nanson thinks that the electors would still have regard for the main parties, even though they grouped themselves into small sections. He declares that "any party amounting to anything like a quota would not only have two candidates of its own—one Liberal and one Conservative—but would also be wooed by candidates of both leading parties." We may well question whether factions would trouble themselves about the main parties; but, granting the assumption, the small parties might just as well be single electorates as far as the main parties are concerned. The Liberal candidates might be successful in all of them, and the Conservatives be unrepresented. The peculiar feature is that the defeated Conservatives are expected to transfer their votes to the Liberals to make up the quotas for the small parties!

The third claim is that electors should have perfect freedom to vote exactly as they please, and yet Professor Nanson, in condemning Mr. Hare's original scheme, has denied that they are free to vote as faddists; but he still holds that they are free to vote on any basis if only they form one-sixth to one-twelfth of an electorate. Thus the amount of freedom is variable and a matter of opinion. Now, we altogether deny that electors should be given the opportunity to subordinate the national interests to factious interests. Just as the faddist argument is fatal to Mr. Hare's original scheme, so the splitting up into factions is fatal to Professor Nanson's present scheme. Where is the freedom which Professor Nanson claims under the present system of election? Is it not the fact that throughout England, America, and Australia the electors have very often a choice between two candidates only—one Ministerialist and one Oppositionist? By all means let us have as many political organizations as possible to make known the wishes of all sections; but the true function of all such organizations is to influence the policies of the two main parties, and not to secure independent delegates in Parliament. This means simply that the compromise among the different sections supporting a party must be effected in the electors' minds, and at the elections, and not on the floor of the Legislature.

The fourth claim is the emancipation of the voters from the tyranny of the "boss." Now, the power of the "boss" lies in the control of nominations, and although to some extent this control is necessary with the present system of election, it is not essential to party government, as we hope to show. But with government by faction there would be no escape from this control. The tyranny of a faction is worse than the tyranny of the "boss." The voters need saving from their own selfish passions far more than from the "boss."

The final claim that each elector is entitled to the full value of his vote, regardless of the way in which it is used, is really a claim to an equality of political power, i.e., to direct government. It means that electors are absolutely free to combine for their own interests, or for their interest as a class, in opposition to the public welfare. These combinations would, with an equality of direct political power, soon bring on social disruption.

Professor Jethro Brown.—In the preface to "The New Democracy," by Professor Jethro Brown, the two fundamental difficulties of present-day politics are correctly stated to be—how to express public opinion, and how to improve its value. For the first of these Professor Brown recommends the Hare system, and for the second the study of history. Later on he writes:—"How is the amelioration of popular sovereignty to be effected? Not, I venture to believe, by the pursuit of the policy which hopes to play off ignorance against ignorance and prejudice against prejudice, and to secure good government by the arts of flattery, manipulation, and intrigue; nor, indeed, by the improvement of democratic machinery, though this is extremely desirable, and calls for immediate attention. For, above all, towers the question of character." It is quite evident that Professor Brown shares the delusion of the other advocates of the Hare system, that the manner of expressing public opinion has nothing to do with the character of public opinion. The two difficulties laid down are essentially one. The cardinal fact underlying representation is that it is a real social force, capable of reacting upon and moulding character, and therefore of improving the value of public opinion. The independence, love of freedom, respect for minorities, and capacity for self-government, which are the most distinctive traits in the English character, are not innate, but are largely the products of the British Constitution. If the only chance of improving the value of public opinion lay in the hope of inducing the individual electors to study the lessons of history, the prospect would be indeed gloomy.

Professor Brown regards party government as a necessary evil, resulting from the mechanical difficulty of securing unity of action from a plurality of wills. This is practically equivalent to saying that legislation itself is a necessary evil. But he writes:—"Whatever may be the evils of party government, there can be no doubt of the utility as well as of the necessity of the institution itself. The alternative to party government is the system of government by small groups. In Australia the evils of this alternative have been occasionally displayed in practical politics; but it is to France that we must look for their supreme illustration." Turning to the chapter on the Hare system, we find that Professor Brown believes that the electors would still divide themselves into two parties, even if given the opportunity to form small groups. "I cannot believe," he writes, "that the reputation of our race for sound common-sense is so far misplaced that a provision for the faithful representation of the people would end in an immoderate Legislature! For, although the Hare system is not perfect, it does undoubtedly afford an opportunity for an absolutely fair representation. Of course the opportunity would be abused by some; but to argue that the abuse would be general, or if at all general, would long continue, is to argue that the people would prove themselves unworthy of the opportunity offered." While he was at the University of Tasmania the first election under the Hare system was held, and Professor Brown's opinions are based on the result. A second election has, however, just been held, which shows the futility of his hopes.

The Tasmanian Experiment.—Despite the fact that it has been advocated for over forty years, the trial now being made of the Hare system in Tasmania is the first application of the "representative principle" to any assembly modelled on the English plan of party government, and therefore deserves more than passing notice. But the experiment is on such a small scale, and has been conducted for such a short time, that the result can hardly be expected to be conclusive as yet. The objection against the Hare system is not so much that it is not suitable to present conditions as that it will speedily bring about altered conditions. It is interesting to find that this is exactly what is taking place. The system is applied in two electorates only, at Hobart and Launceston the former returning six members and the latter four. At the first election, in 1897, the possibilities of the system were not appreciated, and electors voted on the old lines; and although the results were rather erratic and unexpected, they were considered fairly satisfactory. But the second election, held early in the present year, proved a great blow to the system. No less than three of the successful candidates were intensely unpopular; and one of them, an ex-minister, had recently been banished from public life on the report of a select committee of the House. His reinstatement aroused a storm of indignation throughout the colony, and he was forced to retire again before Parliament met. It will be as well to take the evidence of a strong advocate of the system—the Argus correspondent. Of one candidate he writes:—"Judging by all available definite evidences, it seemed that five-sixths of the electors of Hobart were directly in favour of the construction of the railway by the present Great Western Railway Syndicate; while those of the remaining sixth were variously opposed to the company or to the project of constructing such a railway by private enterprise at all. This sixth is represented by Mr. R.C. Patterson, who headed the poll." Of another candidate we learn that "Mr. Mulcahy had fought a hard fight, and it is a fair assumption that on the list of the elected he represents the Roman Catholic vote. As a member of a generally popular Government, the extent of Mr. Mulcahy's personal unpopularity was remarkable and probably unique." But it was over the return of Mr. Miles that the storm raged most. The excuse is made that "the fault of Mr. Miles's return (assuming that it is a fault) lies with the electors who returned him, and not with the system under which his return was accomplished.... Once grant that a section of Hobart electors have the right to select for their representative whom they choose, and it would seem that the Hare system must be held free of all responsibility for the return of Mr. Miles." But this is precisely what cannot be granted for a moment, as we have endeavoured to show. The assertion is made that Mr. Miles would have been returned as easily under the old system, but this is not a fact. He polled only one-eighth of the votes, so that, even supposing that his supporters were twice as strong in a single electorate, he would have had only one-fourth of the votes. It is safe to say, from the small proportion of second and third preferences which he secured, that if the Block Vote had been adopted he would have been at the bottom of the poll. Commenting on these results, the Argus declares that the Hare system does not pretend to reform or guide the people. Very likely not! But is it not quite evident that it has the opposite effect?

Is it too much to say that, if the Hobart experiment be persevered with, the ultimate tendency will be the return of six members, each acceptable to one-sixth of the electors, and obnoxious to the other five-sixths? It is quite obvious already that the usual party lines are entirely disregarded.

Professor Commons.—The best book on the subject yet published is the "Proportional Representation" of John E. Commons, Professor of Sociology in Syracuse University, U.S. Its great merit is that the political and social bearings of the reform are fully treated. Professor Commons rejects the Hare system in favour of the Free List system. He writes:—"The Hare system is advocated by those who, in a too doctrinaire fashion, wish to abolish political parties. They apparently do not realize the impossibility of acting in politics without large groupings of individuals." He makes a great step in advance of the disciples of Mr. Hare in recognizing that the proportional principle should be applied to parties, and not to individuals, and he even defines parties correctly as being based "not altogether on sectional divisions, but on social and economic problems of national scope;" but, unfortunately, he fails to see that there can be only two parties, and that the representation of small parties would not reform the main parties, but break them up altogether. At the same time he is no mere theorist, for he declares:—"If a practicable and effective method of proportional representation cannot be discovered, the theoretical principle is a mere dream." Moreover, he prudently recognizes that his arguments as regards Federal and State Legislatures in America are in advance of what the public is ready to accept, and adds:—"We, as a people are not yet ready to abandon the notion that party responsibility in Federal affairs is essential to safety." His immediate object is, therefore, the reform of city councils, which in America are controlled by the national parties, and are exploited by the notorious "machine" organizations. We may sympathize with this object, for parties in an administrative body are a serious evil, but with legislatures the case is quite different. Professor Commons admits that third and fourth parties, if given their proportionate weight in legislation, would hold the balance of power, but he declares that "the weight of this objection, the most serious yet presented against proportional representation, varies in different grades of government." He then proceeds to examine the objection "as applied to Congress (and incidentally to the State Legislatures), where it has its greatest force, and where pre-eminently party responsibility may be expected to be decisive." And the only answer he can find is that the objection "overlooks the principle of equality and justice in representation. It may prove here that justice is the wisest expediency. It is a curious anomaly, showing confusion of thought regarding democracy, that a people who insist on universal suffrage, and who go to ludicrous limits in granting it, should deny the right of representation to those minor political parties whose existence is the natural fruit of this suffrage." But these minor parties would not be denied representation if they were allowed to exercise freely their true function, which is to influence the policies of the main parties; and it is essential to the working of the political machine that they be limited to that function. Professor Commons continues:—"The argument, however, of those who fear that third parties will hold the balance of power is not based solely on a dread of the corrupt classes, but rather of the idealists, the reformers, 'faddists,' and 'cranks,' so called. They would retain exclusive majority rule and party responsibility in order to prevent the disproportionate influence of these petty groups. They overlook, of course, the weight of the argument already made that individual responsibility is more important for the people than the corporate responsibility of parties." The assumption is here made that the complete suppression of individuality is an essential feature of party government, whereas it is in fact a peculiar feature of American politics, due to "machine" control of nominations. The one point which Professor Commons has missed is that individual candidature can be permitted and representation still be confined to the two main parties.

Conclusion.—The advocates of proportional delegation have failed to grasp the importance of the principles of organization and leadership, which underlie representation. Mr. Hare thought that the effect of doing away with organization would be to improve leadership. But he reckoned without his host—Human Nature. Organization cannot be dispensed with without destroying leadership and bringing on the strife of factions.

FOOTNOTE:
[1] Now Lord Avebury.

THE PRESENT POSITION OF PARTY GOVERNMENT

England.—We have seen that the fundamental error of the proportionalists is that they have failed to distinguish between the two stages of representation. In constantly appealing back to the earlier parliaments they altogether overlook the fact that the functions which Parliament now exercises were then vested in the King. But this error is not confined to the proportionalists, most of whom, indeed, however inconsistently, favour party government. It is also put forth as an argument by those who lay all the blame of present evils on the party system, and who think that all sections should work together as one united party. Take, for instance, the diatribe of Mr. W.S. Lilly on "The Price of Party Government" in the Fortnightly Review for June, 1900. Mr. Lilly complains bitterly that the infallible oracle in politics to-day is "the man in the street." He asserts that all issues are settled "by counting heads, in entire disregard of what the heads contain." His bugbear is the extension of the franchise. "Representative institutions, for example," he asks, "what do they represent? The true theory unquestionably is that they should represent all the features of national life, all the living forces of society, all that makes the country what it is; and that in due proportion. And such was the Constitution of England up to the date of the first Parliamentary Reform Act. Its ideal was, to use the words of Bishop Stubbs, 'an organized collection of the several orders, states, and conditions of men, recognized as possessing political power.'" Could anything be more ridiculous? Political power is to be apportioned in the nineteenth century as it was in the fourteenth century! The people are to be always governed by their superiors! Mr. Lilly continues:—"It appears to me that the root of the

31

falsification of our parliamentary system by the party game is to be found in the falsification of our representative system by the principle of political atomism. Men are not equal in rights any more than they are equal in mights. They are unequal in political value. They ought not to be equal in political power."

The mistake here is in the premise. Has not the demagogue more power than his dupes, or the Member of Parliament more power than the elector? We have hardly yet reached, and are never likely to reach, that ideal of direct government. But what is this price which Mr. Lilly is railing at? "The price may be stated in eight words. 'The complete subordination of national to party interests.' The complete subordination. I use the adjective advisedly. Party interests are not only the first thought of politicians in England, but, too often, the last and only thought." All this is sheer nonsense. The coincidence of party aims with the real interests of the people which the British Parliament has displayed since the Reform Act of 1832 has never been even remotely approached by any other country. Two causes have contributed to this great result; first, the gradual extension of the franchise to all sections of the people, and second, the fact that the principles of organization and leadership have been highly developed. In one respect, however, Mr. Lilly is right. The zenith has been passed. Party government is not the same to-day in England as it was twenty years ago. But the fault lies not with the extension of the suffrage, but with the fact that the principles of organization and leadership are less operative. True, the extension of the franchise is indirectly concerned in the failure, but the primary cause is that the present system of election is unable to bear the increased strain. It no longer suffices to organize the people into two coherent parties. The effect on the parties is correctly noted by Mr. Lilly. "A danger which ever besets them," he declares, "is that of sinking into factions."

Now, the result of the want of organization is the presence in Parliament of small independent factions, which, by holding the balance of power, cause the main parties to degenerate into factions.

This tendency is apparent even in England, and the rock on which the parties have split is the Irish faction. Into the merits of the Irish question we do not propose to enter; it is the career of the faction in Parliament which interests us. But it may be noted that the Irish party rests on a three-fold basis as a faction; it is based mainly on a class grievance, and is also partly racial and partly religious. It was the Irish party in the House of Commons which first discovered that, by keeping aloof from the two main parties, it could terrorize both; and thus found out the weak spot in party government. Its tactics were successful up to a certain point, for Mr. Gladstone succumbed to the temptation to purchase its support, and brought in the Home Rule Bill. The result is known to all; the historical Liberal party was rent in twain; party lines were readjusted; Mr. Gladstone was left in a hopeless minority; and the remnant of his following is to-day in the same condition. What is the lesson to be learned from these events? That these tactics cannot succeed in the long run. All interests suffer, but the culprits most of all. Moreover, such tactics are unconstitutional, and would in some circumstances justify retaliatory measures. Let us trace the constitutional course. The Irish members could have exerted a considerable influence on the policies of both Liberals and Conservatives, just as the Scotch did. If they had followed this course, might they not have been in a better position to-day?

Of course, the Irish faction can hardly be said to be the result of the present system of election; it is mainly the expression of old wrongs. But it has set the example, and the disintegration of the old parties is rapidly proceeding. One feature, however, in connection with the present system in Ireland may be mentioned, and that is the permanent disfranchisement of the minority. In the greater part of Ireland there is no such thing as a contest between the main parties. If a system were introduced by which the minority could get its share of representation the parties would compete on even terms for the support of the people, and good feeling would tend to be restored.

To return to Mr. Lilly. The present position of party government in England is not due to defects in the institution itself, still less to the extension of the suffrage, but to imperfect organization. The true remedy is, therefore, to improve organization, not to restrict the suffrage. By this means such a condition will be brought about that if either party favours a faction it will lose in general favour; then, indeed, we may hope that the main parties themselves will cease to degenerate into factions.

The same number of the Fortnightly contains an unsigned article on "Lord Rosebery and a National Cabinet," in which the party system is alluded to as defunct, and in which the suggestion is thrown out that on the retirement of Lord Salisbury a national cabinet should be formed, comprising both Mr. Chamberlain and Lord Rosebery. Impending foreign complications are given as the excuse for terminating party action. Now, it is not to be denied that party government is more suitable for what Mr. Herbert Spencer calls the industrial type of society than for the militant type. Quite recently Lord Salisbury blamed the British Constitution for the state of unpreparedness for the present war. But it is equally true that in foreign affairs party action is generally suspended: in the control of India, for instance, it is so. The real question, then, is this: Is the danger of foreign aggression so serious that all questions of internal policy can be permanently set aside? If we have reached this stage, the end of modern civilization is in sight. In effect, the proposal is a return to the first stage of representation, with the difference that all sections of the people are expected to be held together by the fear of foreign aggression, instead of the fear of the aggression of the monarchy. Mr. David Syme is a censor of a very different type. So far from wishing to take control from the people, he would give the people absolute control over everything, and at all times. Seldom has the case against party government been more powerfully presented than in his work on "Representative Government in England." But Mr. Syme founds his proposed remedies on a theory of representation which is based on the literal meaning of the word. No one has put the delegation theory more clearly than in the following passage, or gone so far in applying it:—

Representation is a mental act; it is the presentation or reproduction of the state of mind of another person; and before one person can represent another person he must first know what the opinions of that other person are. A representative is a substitute; he stands in the place of, and acts for, another person. But one man cannot act for another unless he knows what that other would do were he acting for himself. In other words, he requires to know the motives which actuate that other person, or what influences his motives, namely, his principles and beliefs. The House of Commons is a representative body, not because every individual member of it represents the opinions of the whole nation, but because members in the aggregate represent those opinions, (p. 170).

This position is diametrically opposed to the principles we have laid down, for it eliminates entirely the ideas of organization and leadership. Again, Mr. Syme says:—"If the government is to be carried on for the benefit of all classes, representatives should be chosen from all classes. We had class representation in the early parliaments, but then all classes were fairly represented." We have shown that the analogy from early parliaments is fallacious. Representatives should now be chosen irrespective of class, and not as class delegates. But Mr. Syme does not carry his theory to its logical conclusion. For if representatives merely express the thoughts of others, and should be class delegates, surely all classes are entitled to have their thoughts "represented;" and Mr. Syme should range himself among the disciples of Mr. Hare. But here comes in an interesting difference. Mr. Syme would retain the present system and make members continually responsible to a majority of their constituents; he would even give this majority power to dismiss them at any time. Now, this is practically an admission that representation involves the existence of a majority and a minority, or, in other words, is a means of organizing the people into a majority and a minority. Again, as regards leadership, the theory will hardly bear the test of facts. Could a man like Gladstone be said to merely express the thoughts of his constituents? Was he not rather a guide and leader of the thoughts of a great part of the British nation?

In addition to the continual responsibility of members to their constituents, Mr. Syme would also make the individual ministers of state responsible to a majority of the members. He adds:—"The whole system of party government could in this manner be quietly and effectively got rid of." We do not propose to criticise the latter suggestion, as we do not believe it would be put forward to-day, in the light of fuller knowledge. Mr. Syme's book was written nearly twenty years ago. But, as regards the continual responsibility of members, we consider it important that the electors should not have their way on single questions. They should periodically express their opinion as to the general line of progress, and the representatives should then have complete control. The necessity for this is to save the people from their anti-social tendencies, which we have already stated as the great objection to all forms of direct government. Lord Macaulay once defined the position exactly in a letter addressed to the electors of Edinburgh. "My opinion," he declared, "is that electors ought at first to choose cautiously; then to confide liberally; and when the term for which they have selected their member has expired to review his conduct equitably, and to pronounce on the whole taken together."

We hope to have left on the reader's mind by this time no doubt as to the intimate connection between the machinery of election and the resulting character of the legislature. Now it is a most extraordinary fact that this connection is hardly noticed by the leading constitutional authorities. It is true they often recognize that suggested changes like the Hare system would debase our legislatures, but it never seems to occur to them that present evils might be cured by a change in the electoral machinery. They point out the evils indeed, but only to indulge in gloomy forebodings at the onward march of democracy, or as warnings of the necessity for placing checks on the people.

Take Bagehot's study of the House of Commons in his standard work on "The English Constitution," where he classifies the functions exercised by the House. He insists that the most important of these is the elective function—its power to elect and dismiss the ministry. In addition, it exercises an expressive function, a teaching function, an informing function, and, lastly, the function of legislation. But not a word is said of the relation of these functions to representation, or to the method of election. It is asserted that the reason the House of Commons is able to exercise these functions is because England is a deferential nation, and the people leave government in the hands of their betters, the higher classes. On one point he is emphatic, and that is the absolute necessity of party. He writes:—

The moment, indeed, that we distinctly conceive that the House of Commons is mainly and above all things an elective assembly, we at once perceive that party is of its essence. The House of Commons lives in a state of perpetual potential choice; at any moment it can choose a ruler and dismiss a ruler. And therefore party is inherent in it, is bone of its bone, and breath of its breath.

As to the present trend of affairs, the opinion of a foreign observer,

Gneist—"History of the English Constitution"—may be quoted:—
England, too, will experience the fact that the transition to the new order of industrial society is brought about through a process of dissolution of the old cohesions, upon which the constitution of Parliament is based. The unrepresented social mass, which is now flooding the substructure of the English Constitution, will only stay its course at a universal suffrage, and a thorough and arithmetical equalization of the constituencies, and will thus attempt, and in a great measure achieve, a further dissolution of the elective bodies. To meet the coming storm a certain fusion of the old parties seems to be immediately requisite, though the propertied classes, in defending their possessions, will certainly not at first display their best qualities. As, further, a regular formation in two parties cannot be kept up, a splitting up into fractions, as in the parliaments of the Continent, will ensue, and the changing of the ministry will modify itself accordingly, so that the Crown will no longer be able to commit the helm of the state in simple alternation to the leader of the one or the other majority. And then a time will recur in which the King in Council may have to undertake the actual leadership. (Vol. ii., pp. 452, 453.)
In other words, that an industrial society is incapable of self-government! Note the reason for this remarkable conclusion—a splitting up into fractions, i.e., imperfect organization.
Take now the evidence of the distinguished historian and publicist, Mr. W.E.H. Leeky, M.P., as given in his recent work on "Democracy and Liberty":—
After all due weight has been given to the possible remedies that have been considered, it still seems to me that the parliamentary system, when it rests on manhood suffrage, or something closely approaching to manhood suffrage, is extremely unlikely to be permanent. This was evidently the opinion of Tocqueville, who was strongly persuaded that the natural result of democracy was a highly concentrated, enervating, but mild despotism. It is the opinion of many of the most eminent contemporary thinkers in France and Germany, and it is, I think, steadily growing in England. This does not mean that parliaments will cease, or that a wide suffrage will be abolished. It means that parliaments, if constructed on this type, cannot permanently remain the supreme power among the nations of the world. Sooner or later they will sink by their own vices and inefficiencies into a lower plane. They will lose the power of making and unmaking ministries, and it will be found absolutely necessary to establish some strong executive independently of their fluctuations. Very probably this executive may be established, as in America and under the French Empire, upon a broad basis of an independent suffrage. Very possibly upper chambers, constituted upon some sagacious plan, will again play a great restraining and directing part in the government of the world. Few persons who have

watched the changes that have passed over our own House of Commons within the last few years will either believe or wish that in fifty years' time it can exercise the power it now does. It is only too probable that some great catastrophe or the stress of a great war may accelerate the change. (Vol. i., pp. 300, 301.)

And the reason assigned for this very unsatisfactory state of affairs is precisely as before:

All the signs of the times point to the probability in England as elsewhere of many ministries resting on precarious majorities formed out of independent or heterogeneous groups. There are few conditions less favourable to the healthy working of parliamentary institutions or in which the danger of an uncontrolled House of Commons is more evident. One consequence of this disintegration of Parliament is a greatly increasing probability that policies which the nation does not really wish for may be carried into effect. The process which the Americans call "log-rolling" becomes very easy. One minority will agree to support the objects of another minority on condition of receiving in return a similar assistance, and a number of small minorities aiming at different objects, no one of which is really desired by the majority of the nation, may attain their several ends by forming themselves into a political syndicate and mutually co-operating. (Vol. i., pp. 152, 153.)

Mr. Lecky, too, holds out very little hope for the future:—

When the present evils infecting our parliamentary system have grown still graver; when a democratic House, more and more broken up into small groups, more and more governed by sectional and interested motives, shall have shown itself evidently incompetent to conduct the business of the country with honour, efficiency, and safety; when the public has learned more fully the enormous danger to national prosperity as well as individual happiness of dissociating power from property and giving the many an unlimited right of confiscating by taxation the possessions of the few— some great reconstruction of government is sure to be demanded. Fifty or even twenty-five years hence the current of political opinion in England will be as different from that of our own day as contemporary political tendencies are different from those in the generation of our fathers. Experience and arguments that are now dismissed may then revive, and play no small part in the politics of the future.

Why make democracy the scapegoat for all these evils, when they are simply due to the imperfect organization of democracy? In any case, the most that could rightly be urged would be that universal suffrage had come before its time. The conclusion that its time will never come is certainly not warranted. Universal suffrage cannot be condemned till it has had a fair trial under a rational system of election. Mr. Lecky appreciates so little the connection between the method of election and the splitting up into groups that he views without alarm the Hare system, which would still further develop groups.

But perhaps no one has caught the spirit of party government more truly than Mr. Lecky. Dealing with the motives which should actuate the statesman, in his latest work, "The Map of Life," he writes:—

In free countries party government is the best if not the only way of conducting public affairs, but it is impossible without a large amount of moral compromise; without a frequent surrender of private judgment and will. A good man will choose his party through disinterested motives, and with a firm and honest conviction that it represents the cast of policy most beneficial to the country. He will on grave occasions assert his independence of party, but in the large majority of cases he must act with his party, even if they are pursuing courses in some degree contrary to his own judgment.

Everyone who is actively engaged in politics—everyone especially who is a member of the House of Commons—must soon learn that if the absolute independence of individual judgment were pushed to its extreme, political anarchy would ensue. The complete concurrence of a large number of independent judgments in a complicated measure is impossible. If party government is to be carried on there must be, both in the Cabinet and in Parliament, perpetual compromise. The first condition of its success is that the Government should have a stable, permanent, disciplined support behind it, and in order that this should be attained the individual member must in most cases vote with his party. Sometimes he must support a measure which he knows to be bad, because its rejection would involve a change of government, which he believes would be a still greater evil than its acceptance, and in order to prevent this evil he may have to vote a direct negative to some resolution containing a statement which he believes to be true, (p. 112.)

Mr. Lecky goes on to point out that "many things have to be done from which a very rigid and austere nature would recoil;" but he adds:—"Those who refuse to accept the conditions of parliamentary life should abstain from entering into it." Moreover, he holds that "inconsistency is no necessary condemnation of a politician, and parties as well as individual statesmen have abundantly shown it." But still "all this curious and indispensable mechanism of party government is compatible with a high and genuine sense of public duty."

The American theory of government is that checks must be placed on a democratic legislature by a fixed Constitution and a separate executive exercising a veto. The late Professor Freeman Snow, of Harvard University, was a strong supporter of this school. His objections to cabinet government are given in the "Annals of the American Academy of Political and Social Science" for July, 1892:—

Cabinet government is the government of a party; and for its successful operation it must have at all times a majority at its back in Parliament. If it were possible to direct the current of public opinion into exactly two channels, there would be but two parties, one of which would generally be in the ascendency; but in practice this is found to be a very difficult thing to accomplish, and it becomes the more difficult as the right of suffrage is extended to the mass of the people, with their ever-varying interests. In the countries of continental Europe parties, if indeed they may be said to exist, are broken up into groups, no two or more of which ever act together for any considerable length of time; and ministries are without a moment's notice confronted at brief intervals with opposing majorities, and must give place to others, whose tenure of office is, however, equally unstable and ephemeral. There is no other alternative; one of the two great parties must yield to any faction which becomes strong enough to hold the balance of power between them, or suffer the inevitable consequences—instability and impotence of government.

Dr. Snow evidently thought that it is not possible to direct the current of public opinion into exactly two channels. He certainly had not the slightest idea that it might be a matter of electoral machinery.

Finally, we may quote the opinion of Mr. James Bryce, M.P., whose "American Commonwealth" is one of the most complete studies of the tendencies of democracy in existence. Comparing the English and American systems, he writes of the former:—

That system could not be deemed to have reached its maturity till the power of the people at large had been established by the Reform Act of 1832. For its essence resides in the delicate equipoise it creates between the three powers, the ministry, the House of Commons, and the people. The House is strong because it can call the ministry to account for every act, and can by refusing supplies compel their resignation. The ministry are not defenceless, because they can dissolve Parliament, and ask the people to judge between it and them. Parliament, when it displaces a ministry, does not strike at executive authority; it merely changes its agents. The ministry when they dissolve Parliament do not attack Parliament as an institution; they recognise the supremacy of the body in asking the country to change the individuals who compose it. Both the House of Commons and the ministry act and move in the full view of the people, who sit as arbiters, prepared to judge in any controversy that may arise. The House is in touch with the people, because every member must watch the lights and shadows of sentiment which play over his own constituency. The ministry are in touch with the people, because they are not only themselves representatives, but are heads of a great party, sensitive to its feelings, forced to weigh the effect of every act they do upon the confidence which the party places in them.... The drawback to this system of exquisite equipoise is the liability of its equilibrium to be frequently disturbed, each disturbance involving either a change of government, with immense temporary inconvenience to the departments, or a general election, with immense expenditure of money and trouble in the country. It is a system whose successful working presupposes the existence of two great parties and no more, parties each strong enough to restrain the violence of the other, yet one of them steadily predominant in any given House of Commons. Where a third, perhaps a fourth, party appears, the conditions are changed. The scales of Parliament oscillate as the weight of this detached group is thrown on one side or the other; dissolutions become more frequent, and even dissolutions may fail to restore stability. The recent history of the French Republic has shown the difficulties of working a Chamber composed of groups, nor is the same source of difficulty unknown in England. (Vol. i., pp. 286, 287.)

Thus we find the opinion unanimously held that the one great fault to which cabinet government is liable is instability of the ministry, owing to imperfect organization of public opinion into two definite lines of policy. Bagehot called it a case of unstable equilibrium, and Bradford, in "The Lesson of Popular Government," goes further when he declares:—"Not to speak disrespectfully, the ministry is like a company of men who, after excessive conviviality, are able to stand upright only by holding on to each other."

Yet, after all, the amount of stability simply depends on the state of organization; and England has demonstrated in the golden period of her political history (about the middle of the present century) that the cabinet form of government can be quite as stable as the presidential form. Therefore, if the present position gives cause for alarm, it is not in the abolition of the cabinet or the restriction of the suffrage that the remedy must be sought, but in improved organization. And this, we hope to show, involves improved electoral machinery.

France.—Turn to France. Is there no lesson to be drawn from the history of that unstable country since the Revolution let loose its flood of human passions, ambitions, and aspirations? Has not every attempt at popular government failed for the same cause—want of organization?

France before the Revolution had groaned for centuries under the burden of a decayed feudalism and an absolute monarchy. The last vestige of constitutional forms had disappeared. The representatives of the estates had not been convened since the meeting of the States-General in 1614. The widespread and unprecedented misery of the people caused them to revolt against being taxed without their consent, and a cry went up for a convocation of the estates. The finances were in such a bad way that Louis XVI. was forced to consent, and the three estates—clergy, nobles, and commons—met at Versailles in 1789. At first they called themselves the National Assembly, but the King foolishly took up such a position with regard to the people's representatives that they swore solemnly that they would not separate till they had laid the foundation of a new Constitution, and henceforth were known as the Constituent Assembly. It was determined that the King should no longer be absolute, and the choice lay between a constitutional monarchy and a republic. The Declaration of the Rights of Man was first drawn up, and the Assembly settled down to its task. The leading spirit was Mirabeau. He had been to England, and had studied the British Constitution, and he rightly saw that France was too distracted by faction to maintain an independent executive. He therefore openly advocated a constitutional monarchy with a cabinet chosen from among the majority of the representatives. But, unfortunately, the Assembly refused to follow his lead; nor would the King take his advice to make a separate appeal to the people. In the midst of the negotiations Mirabeau died, and the last chance of establishing a constitutional monarchy disappeared. The King realized this, and tried to escape to the German frontier but was brought back. He then accepted the new Constitution, and the Legislative Assembly was elected in 1791. From the first it had no elements of stability, being split up into groups, and subject to the fear of the Paris mob. The King continued to plot with the emigrant nobles against the Constitution, and the foreign armies massed on the frontier. The danger brought on the triumph of the revolutionary spirit in 1792. The Paris commune overwhelmed both the King and the Assembly, and the republic was proclaimed. Then followed the execution of the King, the Reign of Terror, the control of the Committee of Public Safety, till finally the anarchy was ended by the military despotism of Bonaparte, who became First Consul and afterwards Emperor.

What is the significance of these events in the light of our previous examination of English history? Simply this: That the French, in passing at once from absolutism and feudalism to complete self-government, were trying to jump to the Second stage of representation without passing through the first stage. Mirabeau was right; the republic was foredoomed to failure because the people had learned neither the power of nor the necessity for organization.

In many respects the French Revolution parallels the English Revolution. In each case the King was beheaded; in each case the anarchy of a disorganized representative body was succeeded by a military despotism; and in each case the monarchy was restored.

It was after the restoration that the English system of party government was developed. Why did this system not now take root in France? Partly because France was not blessed with a king like William of Orange, and partly because the new systeme de bascule, the balance system, in which the king allows each faction in turn to hold the reins of power, was discovered. So, instead of the gradual growth of constitutional liberty which took place in England, the tendency in France was back to absolutism. In 1830 Charles X., finding that he could not manage the Chamber of Deputies, issued the ordinances of St. Cloud, suspending the liberty of the press and dissolving the Legislature. Paris immediately broke out into insurrection, and the King was forced to abdicate. The crown was offered to Louis Philippe, and a second attempt at constitutional monarchy was made. But France was too divided by her unfortunate legacy of faction to maintain a continuous policy. The Legitimists, the Republicans, and the Bonapartists were all awaiting their opportunity. In 1848 the second revolution broke out in Paris; the king fled to England, and a republic was again tried. But the imperialist idea revived when Louis Napoleon was elected President. In 1851 he carried out his famous coup d'etat, and again the Constitution was swept away. In the following year he was accepted as Emperor by an almost unanimous vote. Thus France again elected to be ruled by an irresponsible head. The Third Empire ended with the capture of Napoleon III. at Sedan in 1870, and since then France has carried on her third experiment in republicanism. But still the fatal defect of disorganization retards her progress; the Legislature is still split up into contending factions, and in consequence it has been found impossible to maintain a strong executive. Occasionally the factions sink their differences for a time when their patriotism is appealed to, as they have agreed to do during the currency of the present Exhibition, but it is abundantly evident that France can never be well governed till the people are able to organize two coherent parties. There is ground for hope that the monarchical and imperialist ideas are declining, and that the people are settling down to the conviction that there is nothing left but the republic. What makes recovery difficult is that the national character has been affected by the continual strife in the direction of excitability and desire for change.

Those who wish to understand the forces which brought about the different changes and revolutions, traced by one who has grasped their meaning, should read the account in the first volume of Mr. Bradford's "Lesson of Popular Government." His conclusion only need be quoted here:—

As has been said, that which constitutes the strength of the English. Government, that which has made up its history for the last two hundred years, is the growth and continuity of two solid and coherent parties. Occasionally they have wavered when available leaders and issues were wanting, but as soon as a strong man came forward to take the reins the ranks closed up and the work of mutual competition again went on. On the other hand, the curse and the cause of failure of representative government on the Continent of Europe is the formation within the legislature of unstable and dissolving groups. In France the Extreme Eight, the Eight, the Eight Centre, the Left Centre, the Left, and the Extreme Left are names of differing factions which unite only for temporary purposes and to accomplish a victory over some other unit, but which are fatal to stable and firm government. The same is true of Italy, Spain, and Austria, and if not of Germany it is because military despotism holds all alike in subjection.

Mr. Bodley has come to the same conclusion in his work on "France." He writes:—

There is no restraining power in the French parliamentary system to arrest a member on his easy descent, and he knows that if he escapes penal condemnation he will enjoy relative impunity. Many deputies are men of high integrity; but virtue in a large assembly is of small force without organization, and, moreover, a group of legislators leagued together as a vigilance committee would have neither consistency nor durability, which the discipline of party can alone effect. Corruption of this kind, which has undermined the republic, could not co-exist with party government. A party whose ministers or supporters had incurred as much suspicion as fell on the politicians acquitted in the Panama affair would under it be swept out of existence for a period. When the first denunciations appeared, the leaders of the party, to avert that fate, would have said to their implicated colleagues—"In spite of your abilities and of the manifest exaggeration of these charges we must part company, for though you may have been culpable only of indiscretion, we cannot afford to be identified with doubtful transactions;" and the Opposition, eager not to lose its vantage, would scan with equal keenness the acts of its own members. With party government the electorate would not have appeared to condone those scandals. But as it was, when a deputy involved in them went down before his constituents, whose local interest he had well served, with no opponent more formidable than the nominee of some decayed or immature group, they gave their votes to the old member, whose influence with the prefecture in the past had benefited the district, rather than to the new comer, whose denunciations had no authority; whereas, had each electoral district been the scene of a contest between organized parties, the same spectacle would not have been presented." (Vol. ii., pp. 302, 303.)

Mr. Bodley has, in this last sentence, touched the heart of the problem. If the salvation of France depends on making each electoral district the scene of a contest between two organized parties, is not electoral machinery destined to play an important part in the solution?

The United States.—The third great experiment in representative democracy which the nineteenth century has furnished is that which is being conducted in the United States. The contrast with France is remarkable. Just as France is the supreme example of want of organization, so America is the most conspicuous instance of perfect organization into two great national parties which the world has seen. Yet both experiments were started by a revolution, and practically at the same time. The difference lay in the fact that the Americans inherited the capacity for self-government from their British ancestors, and had already practised it in colonial times, while the French only inherited innumerable causes of dissension.

But organization is not the only characteristic feature of American politics. Strange to say, it is accompanied by a suppression of individuality just as complete. It is organization without responsible leadership. For, in the first place, the politicians look on themselves not as leaders but as followers of the people; and in the second place, there are no leaders in Congress, corresponding to the cabinet ministers of British countries.

Now, the view which we wish to emphasize here is that the present position of American politics is the natural result of the principles embodied in the Constitution adopted in 1789, when the Union was formed. The complete organization and the want of leadership are directly to be traced to the labours of George Washington and his associates. A brief glance at the Constitution and the early history of its working will make this clear.

The thirteen States which revolted from England worked fairly well together under the "Articles of Confederation and Perpetual Union" as long as the war lasted, but as soon as peace was proclaimed it was, as Washington said, no better than anarchy. The famous Convention of 1787 was therefore held, and the Constitution was drawn up. One guiding principle of its framers was to divide power so as to place checks on the will of the people, and on outbursts of popular passion, which were then greatly dreaded. One means of attaining this object was the attempted separation of the legislative and executive functions. We say attempted advisedly, for time has but shown that the two are inseparable. But the framers of the Constitution divided the legislative function between the two Houses, and vested the executive function almost entirely, as they thought, in the President. Montesquieu, in his "Esprit des Lois" had laid down that the great merit of the English Constitution was the separation of these functions, and the Americans accepted this view. But, in truth, the English cabinet system had not then been fully developed. The King was still, not only in appearance, but to some extent also in fact, the head of the executive, and there was nothing to indicate that ministers were so soon to become the real leaders.

The effect of this provision was a struggle between the two branches for supremacy, and the legislatures have won. The President has been degraded to a mere agent, and the legislatures have absorbed the greater part of executive functions, even to the control of finance. Now, the framers of the Constitution were apprehensive that the President might become a mere party agent, and they tried to strengthen his position by two devices. First, they gave him the power to veto statutes unless overruled by a two-thirds majority of Congress; and, secondly, they provided for his election by an electoral college, or by a double system of election. This second provision was designed to ensure the election of a President for personal instead of for party reasons; but it has proved a complete failure. Almost from the first the electoral delegates have had to pledge themselves to support the party nominee. The veto, therefore, has also become practically useless. Thus it has come about that Congress is a body entirely without leaders.

A second defect in the Constitution was that it said nothing about the right of any State to withdraw from the Union. After nearly 70 years this omission was responsible for the Civil War. The legal basis for secession was then abandoned, but combinations of States have since been regarded with the greatest apprehension. This conviction that the Union must be maintained at any price has had very important consequences on the party system. The danger of allowing combinations of States to dominate party lines was demonstrated; and the division of each State by the same national parties was recognized as essential to safety.

In the meantime, as we have seen, Congress had practically got control of the executive functions, which were supposed to be exercised by the President, including the nominations to office. Thus every member of the party in a majority had a share of the plunder, and "the spoils to the victors" became the basis of party organization. The system soon underwent such a remarkable development that nearly 200,000 public offices were at the disposal of the victors at each election. The party organizations immediately became omnipotent. The secret of their power lay in the control of nominations. Each party would nominate one candidate only, and the electors voted neither for men nor measures, but blindly for party. As Mr. Bryce declares:—"The class of professional politicians was therefore the first crop which the spoils system—the system of using public office as private prize of war—bore. Bosses were the second crop."

The development which these party organizations have now reached is extraordinary. Practically we may say that there are only two parties— Republicans and Democrats—and they dominate not only Federal and State politics but also city government. Each party has its list of registered electors, and each holds a primary election before the real election, to decide the party candidate. But these primary elections are a mere matter of form. Only a small fraction of the electors attend them, and only those who have always supported the party are allowed to vote. The nominations are therefore really controlled, by fraud if necessary, by the "ring" of party managers. Generally there is one man who can pull the most strings, and he becomes the "boss." All power is centred in the hands of this irresponsible despot. The men who are elected owe their positions to him, and are responsible to him, not to the public.

Remember that these "machine" organizations have absolute sway in every electorate, from one end of the United States to the other. It may be wondered why the people tolerate them, but they are powerless. Sometimes an independent movement is attempted, but it very rarely succeeds, and even when it does the two "machines" combine against it and agree to divide the spoils. Mr. Bryce writes:—

The disgust is less than a European expects, for it is mingled with amusement. The "boss" is a sort of joke, albeit an expensive joke. "After all," people say, "it is our own fault. If we all went to the primaries, or if we all voted an independent ticket, we could make an end of the 'boss.'" There is a sort of fatalism in their view of democracy. (Vol ii., p. 241.)

What is the meaning of all this wonderful party machinery? It is this: that organization without responsible leadership can only be founded on corruption. In other words, the spoils system is the price which the United States pay for maintaining the Union under the present Constitution. The fault lies ultimately, therefore, in the Constitution, which tends to repress responsible leadership.

Now, the mass of public opinion in America, as Mr. Bryce continually points out, is sound, and attempts have not been wanting to put an end to the system of rotation in public offices. A sustained agitation for civil service reform was entered upon, and the system of competitive examination was applied to a large number of offices. Now at last, the reformers thought, American politics would be purified. But, no! The corruption, simply took a new and more alarming turn. Direct money contributions took the place of the spoils. It became the practice to levy blackmail on corporations either to be let alone, or for the purpose of fleecing the public. The monopolies granted to protected industries are the source of a large share of these "campaign funds." The Legislatures are crowded by professional lobbyists, and it is, in consequence, impossible to obtain justice against the corporations. Surely no stronger proof can be needed that corruption is and must remain the basis of organization so long as there is no responsible leadership.

It would be a mistake, however, to suppose that the Americans are not alive to the failure of their representative institutions. Since Mr. Bryce's great work on "The American Commonwealth" was published two books by American authors have appeared which are very outspoken in condemnation. These are "The Unforeseen Tendencies of Democracy," by Mr. E.L. Godkin; and "The Lesson of Popular Government," by Mr. Gamaliel Bradford. The keynote of the first of these two books is to abolish corruption by destroying the power of the "machine" and the "boss," and of the second to introduce responsible leadership. Mr. Godkin traces the disappearance of distinguished men from public life to the control of all entrance to it by the "machine." The reform of primary elections, he holds, is then the first necessity, since "independent voting" has ceased to be a remedy. But he fails to find a solution. The conclusion he comes to is as follows:—

Is the situation then hopeless? Are we tied up inexorably simply to a choice of evils? I think not. It seems to me that the nomination of candidates is another of the problems of democracy which are never seriously attacked without prolonged perception and discussion of their importance. One of these was the formation of the federal government; another was the abolition of slavery; another was the reform of the civil service. Every one of them looked hopeless in the beginning; but the solution came in each case, through the popular determination to find some better way. (Pp. 92, 93.)

But the evil goes far deeper than Mr. Godkin appears to think. To abolish corruption is to take away the present basis of organization without substituting any other. If irresponsible leadership is to be abandoned, responsible leadership must be introduced. Mr. Bradford's plan, therefore, promises more, for if responsible leadership could be introduced into Congress corruption would then be abolished also.

Mr. Bradford's whole book may be said to be a study of the relations of the executive to the legislature, and the conclusions at which he arrives are a complete vindication of cabinet government. But he finds one fault, and that is the instability of ministries, which he confesses has not been apparent so far in the British House of Commons. He holds, however, that it will become more apparent with the rising tide of democracy. It is rather amusing to find that the greatest obstacle which has to be overcome in proposing a responsible executive is the veneration in which the Constitution is still held and the dislike to copying anything from England. His plan is, therefore, an adaptation of the cabinet to the conditions imposed by the Constitution. He holds that the ministers appointed by the President should sit in Congress and have control of the initiation of legislation. It is to be feared that this would hardly realize the idea of responsible leadership. Mr. Bradford establishes a chain of responsibility by the fact that the ministers are responsible to the President and the President is responsible to the people; but that is a very different thing to the continual responsibility of the cabinet to a majority of the legislature. It is probable that the President's ministers would have to encounter the opposition of a majority in one or both Houses, and it is difficult to see how a deadlock could be avoided. Mr. Bradford contemplates that the people would settle any issues which arise between the two branches at the end of the Presidential term of four years; but it is just as likely that there would then be a new President in any case. We are driven to the conclusion, therefore, that responsible leadership is incompatible with the American system of divided powers and fixed terms of office.

Mr. Bryce comments on the proposal as follows:—

It is hard to say, when one begins to make alterations in an old house, how far one will be led on in rebuilding, and I doubt whether this change in the present American system, possibly in itself desirable, might not be found to involve a reconstruction large enough to put a new face upon several parts of that system. (Vol. i, pp. 290, 291.)

This is very true, but is not a new building required? Is not the old house built on a rotten foundation? Mr. Bradford has certainly overlooked the effect of his proposal on party organization for one thing. If the power over legislation, and especially over expenditure of public money, is to be taken away from the irresponsible committees of Congress, the basis of party organization would cease to be corruption, and both representatives and parties would have to take on an entirely new character. As to the present character of representatives, Mr. Bryce advances a number of reasons why the best men do not go in for politics, such as the want of a social and commercial capital, the residential qualification, the comparative dullness of politics, the attractiveness of other careers, etc, but Mr. Bradford declares that the one explanation which goes further than all these is the absorption of all the powers of the government by the legislature, and the consequent suppression of individuality. He writes:—

The voters are urged to send to Congress men of character, ability, and public spirit. They might as well be asked to select men of that quality to follow the profession of burglars, a comparison which is not intended to convey any disrespect to the number of honest and respectable men who constantly are sent to Congress. Chosen as burglars, they would fail just the same in the business.... It is the organization of Congress which offers every facility to those who wish to buy and those who wish to be bought.

Again, as to the present character of parties, Mr. Bradford declares:—

The names of the two great parties, Republicans and Democrats, have in themselves and at the present time no meaning at all.

Simply because the basis of organization is corruption, and not questions of public policy. For the same reason recent elections have been fought on popular "crazes," such as the silver question. But Mr. Bradford says:—

New parties cannot be formed on constantly changing issues, since to have any strength they must have a certain degree of permanence. The only two nations which have succeeded in forming great national parties are Great Britain and the United States. In other European countries the splitting into groups has almost made representative government impossible.

What Mr. Bradford has failed to appreciate is that the absolutely rigid division into two camps which prevails in America is founded on corruption, and will disappear when corruption is abolished. In the United States such a thing as a Congressman deserting one party for the other is practically unknown. In Great Britain, on the contrary, party lines do continually change as new issues arise; and when they are founded on questions of public policy it must be so. What gives them permanence is that certain principles underlie most questions, and men who have the same political principles are likely to think the same on any single question; and further that a member would rather follow his party and sacrifice his opinion on a single question than sacrifice most of his principles.

Therefore, even if the Americans do succeed in purifying their politics, they will be faced with the same difficulty as exists elsewhere—namely, such improved organization as will secure the return of representatives on questions of general public policy only. The present system of single-membered electorates will not suffice. The only remedy lies in enlarged electorates with electoral machinery which will organize public opinion into two definite lines of policy, and will, by allowing individual candidature merge the primary election into the actual election.

All this involves a radical alteration, both in the Constitution and in the methods of election. But the United States have the great advantage over France that it does not involve also a serious change in the national character. It is not unlikely that some such reform must be brought about before long.

The present position cannot last. The Republican party has so long identified itself with Capital in all its forms, with the protected monopolists, the trusts and the corporations, that the mass of Labour threatens to support the Democrats; and as the latter party maintains the doctrines of direct government and the infallibility of the majority, the result will be such a financial crisis and such an industrial revolution that the Americans will have at last to admit that their government needs total reconstruction.

Australia.—On the first day of the nineteenth century the Union of the Parliaments of Great Britain and Ireland was accomplished; on the first day of the twentieth century Britain's daughters in the southern seas will inaugurate, under her ægis, a new experiment in democracy—the Australian Commonwealth. The time is opportune, then, for a review of the tendencies of Australian politics, and for a comparison with the other great democracies. Thus only can we attempt to cast the horoscope of the new nation.

Australia starts with many advantages over France and America. The science of government is better understood now than when they started; the folly of placing too many checks on the people is recognized; and the British system of responsible leadership by a cabinet in the legislature is fully developed. All these features are embodied in the Constitution, and it only remains for the people to prove their fitness to work it.

Applying the same tests as we have used in the case of the great democracies to the present position of Australian politics, what is the result? First, as regards organization, where do we stand? It must be confessed that we are far behind Great Britain and America, though certainly we are not in the same sad plight as France. Still there is the fact that we are classed among the failures. Take the evidence of Mr. E.L. Godkin in "Unforeseen Tendencies of Democracy:"—

In his Journals during a visit to Turin in 1850, Senior records a conversation with Cesare Balbo, a member of the Chamber in the first Piedmontese Parliament, in which Balbo said, after an exciting financial debate:—"We have not yet acquired parliamentary discipline. Most of the members are more anxious about their own crotchets or their own consistency than about the country. The ministry has a large nominal majority, but every member of it is ready to put them in a minority for any whim of his own." This was probably true of every legislative body on the Continent, and it continues true to this day in Italy, Greece, France, Austria, Germany, and the new Australian democracies. (Pp. 102, 103.)

He adduces in support of the statement the fact that the three colonies of New South Wales, South Australia, and Victoria have had respectively twenty-eight, forty-two, and twenty-six ministries in forty years. Is the prospect any brighter for the new Commonwealth? It is to be feared not, if the present tendencies towards disintegration are allowed to grow. For in the last decade a change has come over Australian politics which portends the gravest danger. We refer to the direct class representation which, under the name of Labour parties, has spread all over the colonies. These so-called Labour "parties" are neither more nor less than class factions. Their policy is everywhere the same—viz., the use of the "balance system," which has proved so disastrous to France. The worst effect is that they prevent the main parties from working out definite policies on public questions, and cause them also to degenerate into factions. In Victoria we have actually had the ludicrous spectacle of the Opposition saving the Government time after time when deserted by its own followers. In New South Wales the individual member is sunk in the party; he must vote as the majority decides. Mr. Reid's term of office was ended by one such caucus. In Queensland, where the party is strongest, it has now practically become one of the main parties, and the whole colony is divided on class lines. Already an Intercolonial Labour Conference has been held, and a pledge drawn up which must be signed by all candidates for the party support at Federal elections. The danger of these tactics is not rightly apprehended in Australia. In reality they mark the first step towards social disruption. We may cite the authority of Mr. James Bryce on this point. After pointing out in "The American Commonwealth" that since the Civil War combinations of States have always acted through the national parties, he writes:—

This is an important security against disruption. And a similar security against the risk of civil strife or revolution is to be found in the fact that the parties are not based on or sensibly affected by differences either of wealth or of social position. Their cleavage is not horizontal, according to social strata, but vertical. This would be less true if it were stated either of the

Northern States separately, or of the Southern States separately: it is true of the Union taken as a whole. It might cease to be true if the new Labour party were to grow till it absorbed or superseded either of the existing parties. The same feature has characterized English politics as compared with those of most European countries, and has been a main cause of the stability of the English government and of the good feeling between different classes in the community. (Vol. ii., p. 38.)

How is it that the public conscience is not alive to the enormity of this anti-social crime? Mainly, we think, because the true principles of representation are not properly understood. It is almost universally assumed that there is no real distinction between direct and representative government. Minorities are tacitly allowed to have as much right to representation as the minority, and the confusion of terms is passed over. The working classes are told by self-seeking demagogues that they are in a majority; that the majority is entitled to rule; and that they have only to organize to come into their heritage. These sycophants, who, as Aristotle of old pointed out, bear the greatest resemblance to the court favourite of the tyrant, ask the people to believe the silly paradox that the united wisdom of the whole people is greater than that of the wisest part. The truth is that no people is fit to exercise equal political rights which is not sensible enough to choose the wisest part to carry on the government, providing only they have control over their selection, and can hold them responsible. Are the working classes in Australia going to demonstrate that they are unfit for the exercise of political rights? Are they going to justify the prognostications of the opponents of popular government? That is the real question at issue. Unless public opinion be aroused to the iniquity of class delegation, the further degradation of Australian politics is inevitable. Let it not be thought that we are decrying the organization of the working classes for political purposes. On the contrary, we hold that the organization of every class and every interest is necessary in order that it shall exert its just share of influence. But the only way in which every class can get its just share is by acting through the two main parties. A class which holds aloof can exert for a short time an undue share of influence, as a faction holding the balance of power, but only at the expense of paralyzing the government.

But the working classes are hardly to be blamed in this matter, for it is a fact that before their action they were not able to exert their just share of influence. The government was such as to promote the rule of private interests instead of the general welfare, and, consequently, their interests were shamefully neglected. The real cause of the mischief was, as in America, the nominating system, which is inseparably connected with the present method of election. The consideration of this question brings us to the second characteristic of Australian politics—namely, the irresponsible leadership of the press.

51

We have seen how in America organization has been effected without responsible leadership in Congress, only at the expense of the irresponsible leadership of the "rings" and "bosses" who control the "machines." In Australia an analogous result has been brought about by different causes. We have not had civil strife to teach us the necessity of organization, nor have we a spoils system available as a basis, but the disorganized state of the legislatures and the consequent weakness of the executive have thrown a large share of leadership into the hands of the press. Both in America and in Australia the prevalence of the ultra-democratic theory that representatives should follow and not lead the people has been a powerful contributing cause. And yet it is as clear as possible that the choice lies between two alternatives. The people must either submit to responsible leadership in Parliament or to irresponsible leadership outside. The ultra-democrats hold that responsible leadership in Parliament is incompatible with popular government. We believe that this is the fundamental error which is leading both the Australian and the American democracies astray. On the contrary, it is the irresponsible despotism which is exercised by the "bosses" in America and the newspapers in Australia which is really incompatible with free government.

The source of the error lies in the failure to grasp the meaning of the term "responsible leadership." It is assumed that either the people must lead and the representatives follow, or the representatives must lead and the people follow. Bagehot may be taken as an exponent of the latter position. He thought that cabinet government was only possible with a deferential nation as opposed to a democratic nation. England he held to be the type of deferential nations, because the people were content to leave the government to the "great governing families"—i.e., to defer to caste, which is in principle the same as deferring to a king, who is supposed to rule by divine right. Mr. Bradford also gives a somewhat exaggerated idea of the importance of the force of personality when he declares that the mass of the people have no "views" on public questions; all they want is to be well governed. The late Professor Freeman Snow, of Harvard University, U.S., was a supporter of the ultra-democratic view. In the "Annals of the American Academy of Political and Social Science" for July, 1892, he declares:—

Mr. Bryce thinks that, "like other crowds, a legislature must be led and ruled." And he has formulated a theory which he believes to be "the essence of free or popular government, and the justification for vesting power in numbers." "Every question that arises in the conduct of government," he asserts, "is either a question of ends or a question of means." And as the "masses are better judges of what will conduce to their happiness than are the-classes placed above them, they must be allowed to determine ends." But, assuming the end to be given, they—the masses—

should leave to their leaders—the trained statesmen—the choice of means. The defect in this theory is that it depends for its successful operation upon the continued "deference of the multitude for the classes placed above them ... upon the principle of noblesse oblige," a principle, by the way, derived from feudal monarchy, which has no existence in the United States, and which ought to be considered a misfortune in any free country....

Mr. Bryce has made a step in advance of Mr Bagehot in trusting the people to determine ends, whatever they may be; why not go one step further, and trust them to determine all questions of policy?

These are the two opposite points of view. They are both equally wrong. The first is simply irresponsible leadership, and the second amounts to the same thing in practice, however much the people may appear to lead in theory. The true position is that the relation between the representatives and the people is reciprocal. Both lead and both follow. The people defer to the representatives, not on account of rank or caste, nor upon the principle of noblesse oblige, but only in so far as the representatives are able to demonstrate their fitness to devise measures for the general welfare. The people, on the other hand, are the ultimate judges, both of measures and of men. This mutual action and reaction constitutes the responsible leadership, which is one of the fundamental principles underlying the device of representation. To it we have already traced the virtue of representation as a social force, capable of moulding national character and of appealing to the higher nature of the people.

An elector who is unable or unwilling to decide grave questions of public policy himself may be a very shrewd judge as to who is best fitted to decide them; and deference to ability is totally different in principle to deference to caste. In a country in the transitional stage between aristocracy and democracy, his judgment may be based partly on the principle of noblesse oblige; but there is not the slightest reason why in a democratic country he should require the representative to defer to him. He will merely require a higher standard and a closer and a more constant demonstration that the measures proposed are conducive to the public well-being. Moreover, it is still necessary that the representatives should be judged periodically on general lines of policy, and that the elector should not have the power of exercising control on single questions. Under these conditions the result of the mutual relation will be an improvement on both sides. But if, under the influence of irresponsible leadership outside Parliament, the people insist on increasing control over their representatives, then not only is Parliament degraded, but progress towards government in the general welfare is stopped.

This long digression as to the real meaning of responsible leadership is necessary in order to gauge the drift of the prevailing tendency towards the irresponsible leadership of the press in Australia. The evil exists in all the colonies, but it is perhaps worse in our own colony of Victoria than in any other country in the world, although it is said to be very bad in Switzerland since the referendum was introduced. We have two morning newspapers in Melbourne, which take opposite sides on nearly every question which arises. They admit into their columns no facts and no arguments which tell against the position they have taken up; nay, more, they resort to downright misrepresentation to support it. It will be said that this is only a form of the party game, but the danger lies in the fact that they circulate in different classes, and therefore these classes see only one side of every question. Moreover, in their competition for the support of classes in which they desire to increase their circulation they use their influence to secure legislation which will appeal to class prejudices, or even undertake a prolonged agitation to relieve special interests from legitimate charges. The Age has for a long time thrived by pandering to the prejudices of the working classes, and especially of the artisans; the Argus now seeks to get even by creating dissension between town and country.

All this interference with the functions of Parliament has a baneful influence on the working of the political machine. The party lines are practically decided by the newspaper contest. We have spoken of the resemblance to the "machine" control over American politics. One of the newspapers is, in effect, managed by a "ring," the other by a "boss." The despotism of David Syme in Melbourne is as unquestioned as that of Richard Croker in New York, or Matthew Quay in Pennsylvania. How close the analogy is may be inferred from the fact that Mr. Syme has exercised, and still claims the right to exercise, control over nominations to Parliament. It is notorious that the ten delegates who "represented" Victoria at the Federation Convention were elected on the Age "ticket." Again, Mr. Syme is known as "the father of protection," and has been able, by the force of his indomitable will, to impose on the colony a tariff which can be compared only to the M'Kinley tariff in America, thus showing that irresponsible leadership in either form is more favourable to the rule of private interests than to the general welfare.

We have said enough to show that in internal affairs the influence of the press, when it directly interferes with Parliament is an anti-social force. In matters of foreign policy the case is still worse. The press is almost universally jingoistic, because it is financially interested in sensationalism. A war generally means a fortune to newspaper proprietors. In such matters, therefore, responsible leadership by Parliament is still more urgently required.

We now come to the claim of those ultra-democrats who preach the poisonous doctrines of direct government and of unrestrained majority rule, that responsible leadership is incompatible with popular government. This claim, is of course, supported by the radical press in Australia. We have already quoted from Mr. Syme's work on "Representative Government in England" the extreme views in which he confuses representation with delegation. "Popular government," he declares, "can only exist where the people can exercise control over their representatives at all times and under all circumstances." The method proposed to obtain this control is to give a majority of the constituents power to dismiss a representative at any time, and is utterly impracticable. Imagine the position of a member elected by a majority of one or two votes! The true way to prevent members abusing their trust is not to increase the direct control of the people, but to prevent the control of the press and all other irresponsible agencies over them; and so to ensure the return of better men.

Perhaps the most striking anomaly in Mr. Syme's position is that, while he would confine the office of Parliament to expressing public opinion, he declares in the same work that "the press at once forms and expresses public opinion."[2] Now, it is quite true that if Parliament is weak and disorganized, or occupies itself in fighting for the spoils of office, the power of forming public opinion is thrown into the hands of the press. But the more power is seized by the press, the more Parliament is degraded, and the less is the chance of recovery. The situation presents little difficulty to Mr. Syme. Every newspaper reader, he declares, "becomes, as it were, a member of that vast assembly, which may be said to embrace the whole nation, so widely are newspapers now read. Had we only the machinery for recording the votes of that assembly, we might easily dispense with Parliament altogether."

These ideas are not of mere academic interest; they have dominated the trend of Victorian politics for many years. The time has now arrived for the people to consider whether it is better to keep a Parliament of weak delegates to express the public opinion which is formed by the press than to elect a Parliament of "leaders of the people," highly-trained legists, economists, and sociologists, to form and direct the public opinion which is expressed by the newspapers. Why should the principle of leadership, as exemplified in Mr. Syme's own career, be given full scope in the press, and entirely repressed in Parliament? As to the kind of influence we mean, no better description could be given than that of the well-known Labour leader, Mr. H.H. Champion. In an open letter to Mr. David Syme in the Champion of 22nd June, 1895, he wrote:—

Yet, if you rose to-morrow morning with the resolve to dismiss the ministry or to reverse the policy of the country, to stop retrenchment or to recommence borrowing, that resolve would infallibly translate itself into fact in a few weeks.

In no country that I know of has any organ in the press so much influence as your paper. It is practically the sole source of information for the majority of the people. It has no competitors. It can make any person or policy popular or unpopular. It can fail to report any man or thing, and for four-fifths of the citizens it is as though that man or thing were not. It can misrepresent any speech or movement, and the printed lie alone will reach the electors. It could teach the people anything you choose. It has ruled the country for a couple of decades. It rules the country to-day.

Professor Jethro Brown shows himself alive to the danger of press domination in Australia. In "The New Democracy" he writes:—"The prestige of Parliament is destroyed when its deliberations and conclusions cease to be the determining factor in legislation. The transfer of the real responsibility for legislation to a new power implies the discrediting of the old school for training leaders." And he quotes with approval the expression of opinion by the Honourable B.R. Wise in the Federal Convention:—

There may be, as Mr. David Syme suggests, no risk involved in the change of masters; but for my part I would sooner trust the destinies of the country to the worst Parliament the people of Australia would elect than to the best newspaper the mind of man has ever imagined.

It is little use, therefore, for the press to further degrade Parliament in the eyes of the people by railing at it in the following terms:—

So it is that Parliament as a working machine is about the clumsiest and least effective that can be conceived of. All our Parliaments are modelled on the necessities of bygone centuries. We want a working Parliament improved up to date; but we lack political invention, and have to jog along with the old lumbering machine—a sort of bullock dray trying to compete with an age of electric railways and motor cars.[3]

The remedy lies with the press itself. Let it abandon all illegitimate influence, and use its power in a legitimate direction to give effect to the principles of organization and responsible leadership in Parliament. But just as the Labour faction cannot altogether be blamed for the present disintegration of Parliament, so the press cannot be held responsible for its degradation. In both eases cause and effect have been interrelated. The mistake which the press has made has been in not perceiving that the more it interferes with the legitimate functions of Parliament, even although with the best intentions, the more it degrades Parliament.

We have now passed in review the two great dangers which assail the Commonwealth at the inception of federation. We have shown how intimately related they are to the two great principles underlying representative government—organization and leadership. Nay, we have seen that all the varied phenomena presented by the great democracies of the world can be expressed in terms of the same two principles.

It remains to show that to give effect to the expression of these two principles in a more perfect manner than ever yet attained is a problem of electoral machinery. This task we shall now undertake.

FOOTNOTES:
[2] "Representative Government in England," p. 123.
[3] Age, 28th June, 1900.

THE REFORM - TRUE PROPORTIONAL
REPRESENTATION

How to give effect to the principles of organization and leadership in an electoral reform—that is the problem which we shall now attempt to solve. We have already laid down the theoretical requirements, which are (1) proportional representation to the two parties—the majority and the minority, and (2) the election by each party separately of its most popular leaders; and we shall now have to consider also how these requirements are modified by practical considerations.

Proportional Representation to the Two Parties, the Majority and the Minority.—It will be as well to illustrate the method proposed by reference to the conditions imposed by an actual election, such as that for the Federal Senate. The Commonwealth Bill provides that each State shall be polled as a single electorate, returning six senators. Suppose that 120,000 electors vote on party lines in any State. It is clear that a party which has the support of 20,000 electors is entitled to one senator; also, that a party which has the support of 40,000 electors is entitled to two senators; of 60,000 electors to three senators, and so on. Now, suppose that one party has the support of 50,000 electors, and the other of 70,000 electors, then the minority is entitled to two and a half senators, and the majority to three and a half senators. But senators are living units, and cannot be divided into fractions. The question therefore arises, Which is entitled to the odd senator, the majority or the minority? And the answer is that they are both equally entitled to him; for it is as much a tie as if each party has the support of 10,000 electors in a single-seat electorate. But if the minority had the support of 49,999 electors, or one elector less, it would be entitled to only two senators, and if it had the support of 50,001 electors, or one elector more, it would be entitled to three senators.

From the above simple facts can be deduced general rules applicable to any particular case. It is evident that the result is not affected by the number of votes allowed to each elector, providing only that each elector has the same number of votes. It is also quite irrespective of the number of candidates nominated in the interests of each party. But it would never do to allow party organizations to control nominations. How are we to combine individual candidature with party nomination? The only way to do this is to require that each candidate shall declare, either when nominating or a few days before the election, on which side of the House he intends to sit, and be classified accordingly as Ministerialist or Oppositionist. To decide the relative strengths of the two parties, it is then only necessary to take the aggregate votes polled by all the candidates nominated for each party as a measure of the amount of support which it receives.

The great advantages of this provision are at once apparent. There is no incentive to limit the number of candidates so as to prevent splitting the votes. On the contrary, it is to the interest of each party to get as many strong candidates as possible to stand in its interests. There will be no necessity to ask any candidate to retire for fear of losing a seat to the party. Thus the control of nominations, which leads to the worst abuses of the present system, will be entirely obviated.

Now, suppose that in the instance we have already given each elector is allowed to vote for one candidate only, the total number of votes recorded will be 120,000. Then the unit of representation or number of votes which entitle a party to one senator will be 20,000 votes; each party will be entitled to one senator for every whole unit of representation, and the odd senator will go to the party having the larger remainder. For instance, if the aggregate votes polled by all the Ministerialist candidates be 72,000, and by the Oppositionist candidates 48,000, the Ministerialists, having three units plus 12,000 remainder, are entitled to four senators, and the Opposition, having two units plus 8,000, to two senators.

Similarly, if each elector be allowed to vote for a number of candidates, all these figures will be increased in proportion. For example, if each elector has three votes, the unit of representation would be 60,000 votes. The following general rules may therefore be stated:—

1. The unit of representation is equal to the total number of valid votes cast at the election, divided by the number of seats.

2. Each party is entitled to one seat for every whole unit of representation contained in the aggregate votes polled by all its candidates, and the odd seat goes to the party which has the larger remainder.

The fact that the last seat has to be assigned to the party which has the larger remainder is sometimes advanced as an objection, but it is evidently the fairest possible division that the size of the electorate will permit. Of course, the larger the electorate the more accurately proportioned will be the representation. Hence the representation would be most accurate if the whole assembly were elected in one large electorate. But if, for the sake of convenience, the assembly be elected in a large number of electorates in which the relative proportions of two parties vary the gains which a party makes in some electorates will be balanced by losses in others, so that the final result would be almost as accurate as if the whole country were polled as one electorate. It must be remembered that the result in any electorate cannot be foreseen, and that it is a matter of chance which party gains the advantage. Now, if the limits of variation comprise even a single unit of representation, each party will stand an equal chance of gaining, and therefore the laws of chance will ensure that the gains balance the losses in the different electorates. Supposing a party which averages 40 per cent. in the whole country to vary between 30 per cent. and 50 per cent, in the different electorates (which may be taken as a fair assumption), the unit of representation should equal 20 per cent., or one-fifth. Under these conditions the laws of chance will ensure correct representation, so long as the electorates do not contain less than five seats.

The above facts furnish a complete answer to the arguments advanced by Mr. J.W. M'Cay, ex-M.L.A., in a series of articles in the Age against the application of proportional representation to the Federal Senate. While apparently recognizing that it is utterly impossible for the minority to secure a majority of the representation, he based his objection solely on the fact that a minority is able with electorates containing an even number of seats to secure one-half of the representation, and thus lead to what he terms "the minority block."

The force of the objection will entirely depend on the size of the minority which is able thus to thwart the will of the majority. The Federal Senate will consist of 36 senators, each of the original States contributing six. No reasonable man would complain if the minority, being only entitled to 17 senators, actually returned 18, but Mr. M'Cay points out that it is possible for a minority entitled to 15 senators to return 18. To bring about this result he makes the absurd assumption that in each of the six States the minority polls exactly two whole units of representation, and a bare majority of a third unit. It is safe to say that this would not happen once in a thousand years. If the relative proportions of the two parties vary in the slightest in the different States some must be under and some over the assumed proportion. It is most probable that it will be under it in three States and over it in the other three States; and, under these circumstances, the party will return 15 senators, the exact number to which it is entitled. It may happen to be under the assumed proportion in only two of the States and over in the other four, and that the party will get one more senator than it is entitled to; but it is extremely improbable that it will get two more, and virtually impossible that it will get three more senators than its just proportion. Mr. M'Cay's conclusion that proportional representation can only be used in electorates returning an odd number of representatives is shown to be entirely unwarranted. Equally fallacious is Professor Nanson's rebutting statement that "scientific proportionalists recommend odd electorates." While the number of States remains even, the mathematical chance of a minority securing one-half of the representation is precisely the same whether the States return an odd or an even number of senators. As a matter of fact, the danger of a minority securing one-half of the representation is much greater at the intermediate elections for the Senate, when each State returns three senators, the reason being the smaller field.

We have dwelt at some length on the preceding example, because it serves to refute another error into which some of the proportionalists have fallen. It is held that the unit of representation should be ascertained by dividing the total votes, not by the number of seats, but by the seats increased by one. This unit is generally known as the Droop quota, having been proposed in a work published by Mr. H.R. Droop in 1869. Since one vote more than one-half of the total votes is sufficient for election in a single-seat electorate, it is argued that one vote more than one-third suffices in a two-seat electorate, one vote more than one-fourth in a three-seat electorate, and so on. The unit in a six-seat electorate would be one-seventh of the votes instead of one-sixth, and it is pointed out that by this means the whole six seats would be filled by whole units, leaving an unrepresented residuum of one-seventh of the votes divided between the two parties.

The error lies precisely as before in concentrating attention on one of the electorates, and in neglecting the theory of probability. The Droop quota introduces the condition that each party must pay a certain minimum number of votes for each seat, and the real distinction is that, instead of the minority and the majority having an equal chance of securing any advantage, the chances are in the same proportion as their relative strengths. If the majority be twice as strong as the minority, it will have twice the chance of gaining the advantage. To prove this, consider the position of a one-third minority in a number of five-seat electorates. The Droop quota being one-sixth of the votes, the minority will secure two seats or 40 per cent. in those electorates where it is just over one-third, and one seat or 20 per cent. where it is just under. Since the mathematical chances are that it will be over in one half and under in the other half, it will, on the average, secure only 30 per cent., although entitled to 33 per cent. Again, if the 670 members of the House of Commons were elected in three to five-seat electorates, and the Droop quota used as proposed by Sir John Lubbock, and if the Ministerialists were twice as strong as the Oppositionists, they would, on the average, return 30 more members than the two-thirds to which they are entitled, and this would count 60 members on a division.

The following table illustrates the erroneous result obtained by applying the Droop quota when a number of grouped-electorates are concerned. It will be noticed that where parties are nearly equal it makes very little difference which unit is used:—

STRENGTH OF PARTY	AVERAGE REPRESENTATION	
	Five-Seat Electorates	Ten-Seat Electorates
10 per cent.	6 per cent.	2 per cent.
20 per cent.	14 per cent.	17 per cent.
30 per cent.	26 per cent.	28 per cent.
40 per cent.	38 per cent.	39 per cent.
50 per cent.	50 per cent.	50 per cent.

The Droop quota, therefore, gives, not proportional, but disproportional representation.

Election by Each Party of its Most Popular Candidates.—Still keeping in mind the six-seat electorate for the Federal Senate, we may note that there are two rival systems in the field—the scrutin de liste or Block Vote, in which each elector votes for any six of the candidates, and the Hare system, which allows each elector an effective vote for one candidate only. The adoption of either of these systems would be unfortunate. To force each elector to vote for six candidates is probably to require him to vote for more than he is inclined to support, and certainly for more than his party is entitled to return; and, also, to put it in the power of the majority to return all six senators. To allow him to vote for one candidate only, on the other hand, is to break up both parties into factions by allowing the favourites of sections within the parties to be elected, instead of those most in general favour with all sections composing each party. An intermediate position is therefore best. No elector should be required to vote for more than three candidates, and no elector should be allowed to vote for less. Because in the first place it is evident that each party will, on the average, return three senators, and, secondly, it may be taken for granted that even the minority will nominate at least three candidates. Two alternative proposals may be submitted as fulfilling these conditions:—

1. Each elector should vote for any three candidates, or
2. Each elector should have six votes, and have the option of giving two votes to individual candidates.

The first plan is the simpler, but the second is probably the better, as it allows more discrimination without sacrificing any of the advantages. Either proposal is practically equivalent to applying the Block Vote to each party separately; and whatever may be the objections to applying the Block Vote to two or more parties it is the simplest and best system to elect the candidates most in general favour when one party only is concerned. It is true that the majority will return rather more than one-half of the representatives and the minority rather less than one-half, so that the minority will have more votes in proportion to its strength. But with two parties of fairly equal but fluctuating strength the fairest way is to require each elector to vote for at least one-half of the number of representatives. Besides, apart from the fact that it is not known before the election how many seats each party will obtain, it is absolutely necessary that each elector shall have the same number of votes in order that each party be allotted its just share of representation. Moreover it is not proposed to limit the elector's freedom of choice in the slightest by confining him to the candidates of one party. The great majority of electors will vote on party lines, because every vote given to a candidate of the opposing party tells against the representation of their own party. The reason of this is that every vote counts individually for the candidate and collectively for the whole party. Any elector, therefore, who divides his voting power equally between the two parties practically wastes it as far as the party representation is concerned. But it is neither necessary nor desirable to bring about such a rigid party division as prevails in America, for instance, where a man is born, lives, and dies Republican or Democrat. If electors were confined to the candidates of one party, an elector who wished to vote for an individual candidate of the opposing party would be placed in the dilemma of deserting either his favourite or his party. The division into parties is really required in the elected body, and not in the constituent body.

Rules for the Reform.—We are now in a position to draw up a list of rules for the proposed reform, applicable to all legislatures in which party government prevails:—

1. Electorates to be grouped so as to contain at least three seats, and preferably not less than five seats nor more than twenty seats.

2. Candidates to declare when nominating, or a few days before the election, whether they are in favour of or opposed to the party in power, and to be classified accordingly as Ministerialists or Oppositionists.

3. Ballot papers to contain the names of all candidates nominated, arranged in two parallel columns, one headed Ministerialists, and the other Oppositionists. The list of candidates under each heading to be arranged in alphabetical order.

4. Each elector to have as many votes as there are seats, and to be allowed to give either one or two votes to any candidate. The votes to be distributed as he pleases among all the candidates of both lists.

5. The total number of valid votes cast at the election to be divided by the number of seats; the quotient to be known as the "unit of representation."

6. Each party to be allowed one seat for every whole unit of representation contained in the aggregate votes polled by all its candidates, and the last seat to go to the party which has the larger remainder.

7. The candidates of each party having the highest number of votes to be declared elected to the number of seats to which each party is entitled in accordance with the preceding rule.

8. In case of a tie between candidates or parties the lot decides.

The alternative plan for rule 4, which is somewhat simpler, would read as follows:—

4. Each elector to vote for half the number of candidates that there are seats, i.e., three votes in a five or six-seat electorate, four votes in a seven or eight-seat electorate, andc. The votes to be distributed as he pleases among all the candidates of both lists.

It is unnecessary to dwell on the absolute simplicity of these rules. They involve no radical departure from existing methods of voting or of counting votes. Once the totals are added up, the calculations necessary to decide the successful candidates are within the reach of a school child.

EXAMPLE.—Take as an example 13 candidates in a six-seat electorate who poll as follows:—

MINISTERIALISTS.
OPPOSITIONISTS.
BROWN 83,000 YOUNG 53,000
RYAN 74,000 BELL 51,000
COX 44,000 HUME 47,000
WHITE 42,000 JONES 45,000
PEEL 38,000 BLACK 34,000
ADAMS 35,000 ---------
230,000
GREY 33,000
SWIFT 21,000

370,000

Total votes = 370,000 + 230,000 = 600,000.

Unit of representation = 600,000/6 = 100,000.

Ministerialists: 3 units + 70,000 remainder = 4 seats.

Oppositionists: 2 units + 30,000 remainder = 2 seats.

The Ministerialists, having the larger remainder, secure the last seat. The successful candidates are Brown, Ryan, Cox, and White (M.), Young and Bell (O.)

It will be noted that without the proportional principle the Ministerialists would have returned two members only, and the Oppositionists four.

It is to be distinctly understood that the simpler plan of voting for half the number of candidates that there are seats is practically as good as the other.

In order to show, however, that the plan we have favoured may be simplified, we illustrate by a sample ballot paper a method which has been used in Belgium. Two white spots are printed opposite each candidate's name. An ink pad and stamp are then provided at each polling booth, and the elector stamps out a white spot for each vote he wishes to give. In the paper illustrated two votes are given to Brown, two to Jones, one to Grey, and one to Swift. This elector has, therefore, given two-thirds of his voting power to the Ministerial party, and one-third to the Opposition, and has thus directly influenced both policies. A further advantage of the proposal is the ease with which such a paper can be read by the returning officer.

BALLOT PAPER

Ministerialists.　　Oppositionists.

O　O ADAMS O　O BELL

BROWN O　O BLACK

O　O COX O　O HUME

O　　GREY JONES

O　O PEEL O　O YOUNG

O　O RYAN

O SWIFT

O　O WHITE

1. You are allowed Six votes, and can give either one or two votes to any candidate on either list.

2. Stamp out one of the white spots if you wish to give a candidate one vote.

3. Stamp out the two white spots if you wish to give a candidate two votes.

4. Your ballot paper will be invalid if you stamp out more or less than Six white spots.

Character of Parties.—We must now prove that the methods proposed will actually organize the people into two coherent parties. Let us suppose either party to be composed of three sections. The problem is to induce these three sections to work together, and to sink their petty differences in the general interest, in short to unite as a party, aiming at the control of administration with a definite policy on public questions. Let us further suppose the party entitled to three representatives. Now, it is quite conceivable that exactly the same three candidates would be elected if each elector had any number of votes from one to three, and this would actually tend to be the case the more united the party is. But herein lies the difference: that with one vote only any one section holding narrow and violent views can return an independent delegate, and therefore has a direct inducement to do so, while with three votes it is forced to work with the other two sections, for if it refuses to do so it is in their power to exclude its nominee. It is this power to exclude independent factions which is the first requisite to prevent the main parties degenerating into factions. Now, the advocates of the Hare system declare that each elector should have one effective vote only, no matter how many seats the party is entitled to. The elector would therefore only express his opinion as to the delegate of his own section, and not as to the constitution of the whole party, and there would be nothing whatever to prevent the election of the favourites of sections, instead of the representatives most in general favour with all sections.

But if there were only one party it would be impossible to make all the sections work together in this manner. Some of them would combine into a majority of the party, and would exclude the minority. With two great competing parties, however, the case is quite different. So far from either party wishing to exclude any small minority, both will compete for its support, providing only that it will fall into line with the other sections on the main questions of policy. Each section will therefore support the party which will consent to embody the most favourable compromise of its demands in its policy. If its demands are such that both parties refuse to entertain them, it will exercise no influence in the direction of furthering its own views. From this statement it is evident that no system of independent direct proportional representation within the party can be recognized as a right to which the different sections are entitled, as it would inevitably break up the party, and lead to sectional delegation. The sections would then change in character, and become violent factions. But, nevertheless, if the sections work together as described, every section will be proportionately represented in the party policy, and therefore by every representative of the party. Moreover, no section can dictate to either party, or obtain more than a fair compromise. For all the sections are interdependent, and any section which attempts to exert more than its just share of influence will sink in general favour, and will find those who are inclined to support its pretensions rejected at the election.

The difference between the two stages of representation may now be clearly appreciated. In the first stage we have seen that the fear of the aggression of the monarchy held all sections together in one party. In the second stage, however, it has been abundantly demonstrated by experience that the fear of each other will not hold the sections of the two parties together. The electoral machinery must, therefore, supply the deficiency.

Party Lines.—With the altered character of parties there is ground for hope that the basis of division will become questions of general public policy, and that all causes of factious dissension and of social disruption will tend to be repressed. This improvement is indeed urgently needed. For if in any country party lines are decided by geographical considerations, as town v. country; by class, as Capital v. Labour; by race as in South Africa; by religion as in Belgium; or by personal ambition for the spoils of office—in any of these cases the future of that country is open to the gravest doubt.

Perhaps the greatest danger which assails most democratic countries to-day is the risk of the working classes being persuaded by demagogues that equal political rights have been extended to them in order that they shall govern, instead of in order that they shall not be misgoverned. If the general welfare is to be advanced, all classes must influence the policies of both parties. This condition is indispensable to bring about the ideal condition of two parties differing only as to what is best for all.

Equally to be condemned is the narrow-minded and intolerant view of those who can see no virtue in an opposing party; who define, for instance, the distinction between parties as the party for things as they are, and the party for things as they ought to be; the latter being, of course, their own party. This is one of the objectionable features of Australian newspaper-made politics.

A more rational view of the distinction which often underlies party divisions is between those who desire change and those who oppose change. J.S. Mill points out how the latter may often be useful in preventing progress in a wrong direction. There are times when such attitude is called for, but generally speaking we may say that the fundamental distinction between parties should be a difference of opinion as to the direction of progress. Nor is it inconsistent for a party to change its opinion or alter its policy; on the contrary, it is essential to progress. The majority must often modify its policy in the light of the criticism of the minority, and the minority must often drop the unpopular proposals which have put it in a minority. These features are all essential to the working of the political machine.

The Character of Representatives.—Granting that all sections of each party can be induced to work together, the beneficial effect on the character of representatives would be incalculable. Instead of being forced to pander to every small section for support, they would appeal to all sections. The enlarged electorates which are contemplated would be arranged to embrace the widest diversity of interest, and a representative would then be free to follow his own independent judgment, unfettered by the dictation of small cliques. His actions might offend some sections who supported his election; but he has a wide field, and may gain the support of other sections by them. Therefore, he may actually improve his position by gaining more supporters than he loses. Contrast this with the present system, in which the representatives are cooped up in single-membered electorates to denned sets of supporters. The very principle of community of interest on which these electorates must be arranged in order to get a fair result is destructive of the idea of representation. It is no wonder, then, that the present system is tending towards delegation. Local delegation we have always had, more or less, but we are now threatened by class delegation also.

The conclusion of Mr. Kent in "The English Radicals" may be quoted on this point. He says:—

The question of the relationship of members to their constituents is at the present time perplexed and undetermined; for though the control of Parliament by the people is an indisputable fact, yet it is maintained by means of quite another kind from those which the early Radicals proposed. The result is somewhat paradoxical, for while the system of pledges has been contemptuously rejected, yet the theory that a member is a delegate tacitly prevails in English politics. That members of the House of Commons have tended and do tend to lose their independence it is impossible to doubt. A distinguished French publicist, M. Boutmy, for instance, has remarked the fact; and he thinks that in consequence a deterioration of the tone of politicians is likely to recur. Mr. E.L. Godkin, an American writer, whose judgments are entitled to respect, has expressed much the same opinion; "the delegate theory," he says, "has been gaining ground in England, and in America has almost completely succeeded in asserting its sway, so that we have seen many cases in which members of Congress have openly declared their dissent from the measures for which they voted in obedience to their constituents."

It is one of the greatest merits of the proposed reform that this vexed question of representation or delegation would be definitely settled. For, although the area of independent action is enlarged, definite limits are set to it.

Possible Objections.—We may now reply to some objections which have been or might be urged. At the outset we would point out that the critics nearly always base their objections on the conditions which have prevailed in the past or do exist in the present chaotic state of parties; and seldom appreciate the fact that they would lose force if a better condition could be brought about. Let us take the Melbourne Argus report of Professor Nanson's objections:—

Professor Nanson pointed out that the scheme depended for its efficacy on the existence of party government, which the Professor was glad to say was being pushed more and more into the background. He took a practical illustration from the defeat of the O'Loghlen Government in 1883. In that case, after the election the Government came back with a following of one-tenth. The other combined party had nine-tenths, and of these a little more than half were Liberals and a little less than half were Conservatives. He pointed out that under Mr. Ashworth's system the Liberals would have got the whole of the Opposition seats and the Conservatives none, whereas under any intelligent modification of the Hare system the parties would have been returned in the proportion of five Liberals, four Conservatives, and one O'Loghlenite. The system contained the evils of the scrutin de liste doubled by being applied to two parties, the evils of the Limited Vote, which had been condemned by all leading statesmen, and it played into the hands of these who were best able to organize.

Take the latter statements first. The evil of the Block Vote or scrutin de liste is that it gives all the representation to the majority, and excludes the minority; its merit is that it prevents the formation of a number of minorities. How this evil will be doubled if it is entirely removed by allowing both majority and minority their just share of representation we leave the Professor to explain. The statement that the scheme would play into the hands of those who are best able to organize is absolutely without foundation. On the contrary, the organization is automatic. It would certainly encourage the formation of organizations to influence the policies of the parties, since every organization would be able to exert its proportionate influence, but that is an advantage, not an evil. We will leave the statement about party government alone, and now take the "practical illustration." The Professor here assumes three distinct parties, but it is quite evident there are only two. It is not usual for Liberal Unionists and Conservatives to fight one another at elections in Great Britain at present. In the same way, if a section of Liberals and a section of Conservatives unite to oppose a Government, they will work together and not try to exclude one another. Moreover, they will have a common policy, so that it matters little who are elected so long as they are the best men to carry out the policy. Is it likely the Conservatives would join the Liberals, if the latter were trying to get all the seats? Thus all the Professor's assumptions are incorrect. But even if they were correct the conclusion is still wrong. The Liberal section could not get all the seats if they tried. Imagine a ten-seat electorate, in which the combined party is entitled to nine members. The electors would not be required to vote for more than five candidates, whereas the Professor has assumed that they would be forced to vote for nine. He has forgotten that the Block Vote becomes the Limited Vote under the conditions named, and that the Limited Vote allows the minority a share of representation. Besides, in any case, these conditions would never arise in a country in a healthy state of political activity, because then parties would tend more nearly to equalize each other in strength.

It has also been objected that a Ministerialist candidate, say, might stand as an Oppositionist, if the votes of the Opposition candidates were more split up and it was likely to require less votes for election in that party. This is a rather fantastic suggestion. The candidate in question would have to declare himself in favour of a number of things which he would oppose immediately he was elected. If not, he would have to openly declare his intention, but that could easily be made illegal. In any case there would be very little gained, and there is further the risk that, if defeated, all his votes would count to the Opposition.

Another possible objection is that too many candidates might stand, since it is to the interest of each party to get all the support it can. But candidates are not likely to stand to oblige the party or when there is no chance of being elected. It is quite possible that, in a country already split up into numerous groups, the groups would refuse to act together, and that each group would nominate its own list. This is an extreme assumption, and certainly would not happen in British countries. And there would be a constant incentive to the groups to compromise, since a combination can return its candidates.

We hope now to have at least established the fact that the organization of a democracy into two coherent parties—a majority and a minority—is vitally connected with the electoral machinery. We do not claim that the method we have proposed will induce a people to vote on true party lines all at once, for human nature cannot be changed in a day; but we do confidently assert that it will greatly accelerate that desirable result, and will tend to give effect to the principles of organization and responsible leadership.

HOW THE EVILS OF THE PRESENT SYSTEM WILL BE REMEDIED

From the inception of the representative system it has been usual to elect representatives in small districts, returning only one or two members, and the single-membered electorate is now almost universal. In the early Parliaments, however, elections were not contested as they are nowadays. It was merely a choice of the most suitable men to represent a corporate local community. Hence an indirect method of election was generally resorted to, the final choice being left to a small committee of the most important men. With the gradual rise of the party system the conditions entirely changed; and it is important to gain a clear idea of what is involved in the change.

In the first stage we have referred to it is not probable that there were any candidates at all. The position of member of Parliament was not sought after; it was rather thrust upon the man selected as a duty he owed the community. The choice would usually be unanimous, since there would be some men whose recognized influence and attainments would mark them off as most fitted for the position. If there was any difference of opinion it would be merely as to who was best fitted to represent all, and therefore there would never be any excluded minority.

The essential difference in the second stage is that every election is contested by two organized parties. The choice is now not of men only, but of measures and of men as well. It is a contest in the first place within each party as to who is best fitted to represent the party, and in the second place between the two parties for the support of the people. The party in a majority secures all the representation; the party in a minority none. Now, the minority is certainly not represented by the choice of the majority; on the contrary, its views are exactly the opposite. Hence the question arises: Is not this exclusion of the minority an injustice? Does it not amount to disfranchisement? The usual reply is either that the majority must rule or that the injustice done in some electorates is balanced in others, so that in the long run rough justice is obtained.

As to the first contention, it is the party which has the support of a majority of the whole people which should rule; and the excluded minority in some of the electorates belongs to this party. The second practically amounts to the statement that two wrongs make a right.

A practice prevails in the United States which will illustrate the position. Each State sends a number of representatives to Congress proportional to its population, and the division into electorates is left to the State. By manipulating the electoral boundaries the party which has a majority in each State is enabled to arrange that the injustice done to itself is a minimum, and that the injustice done to the opposing party is a maximum. By this iniquitous practice, which is known as the gerrymander, the party in a minority in each State is allowed to get only about one-half or one-quarter of its proper share of representation. But as the practice is universal in all the States, the injustice done to a party in some States is balanced in others. Will those who seek to excuse the injustice done to the minority in each electorate by the present system of election seriously contend that the same argument justifies the gerrymander?

The truth is that the present system has survived the passage from the first stage of representation into the second, not because it does justice to both parties, but because it has operated largely to prevent the formation of more than two parties. It has, therefore, been a means of giving effect to the central feature of representation, viz.: the organization of public opinion into two definite lines of policy. But it is a comparatively ineffective means, and it no longer suffices to prevent sectional delegation in any of the democracies we have examined. Besides, it is accompanied by a series of other evils, which in so far as they lead to the suppression of responsible leadership, tend to the degradation of public life. We propose now to consider the effect of the reform in remedying these defects of the present system.

Parties Not Represented in the Legislature in the Same Proportion as in the Country.—Representation under the present system is purely arbitrary; the amount which each party secures is a matter of chance. If a party with a majority in the whole country has a majority in each of the electorates it will secure all the representation. On the other hand, if it splits up its votes in each electorate, or even only in those electorates where it has a majority, it may secure none at all. Theoretically, then, any result is possible. The argument would lose its force, however, if in practice the result usually came out about right. But this seldom happens, and, speaking generally, two cases may be distinguished: first, when parties are nearly equal, the minority is almost as likely as the majority to return a majority of the representatives, thus defeating the principle of majority rule; and, second, when one party has a substantial majority, it generally sweeps the board and annihilates the minority. A few examples will illustrate these facts.

The 1895 election for the Imperial Parliament is analyzed by Sir John Lubbock in the Proportional Representation Review. He shows that out of 481 contested seats, the Liberals, with 1,800,000 votes were entitled to 242, and the Conservatives and Liberal Unionists, with 1,775,000 to 239, a majority of three seats for the Liberals. But the Conservatives and Unionists actually returned 279, and the Liberals only 202, a majority of 77 seats. The Conservatives and Unionists obtained also a majority of 75 of the uncontested seats, giving them a total majority of 152, instead of the 72 to which they were entitled.

Recent elections for the United States Congress are shown by Professor Commons to present striking inequalities. At the election for the 51st Congress, 1888, the Republicans polled 5,348,379, and the Democrats 5,502,581. But the Republican minority actually secured 164 seats against 161, a majority of 3, and were enabled to carry the McKinley tariff law. For the 52nd Congress, 1890, the Republicans, with 4,217,266 votes, only elected 88, while the Democrats, with 4,974,450 votes, elected 235, and the Populists, with 354,217 votes, elected 9 Congressmen. The Democratic majority should have been only 2, instead of 138. Compared with the 51st Congress, their proportion of the popular vote increased only 1 per cent., but their proportion of the representatives increased 21 per cent. It required 47,923 votes to elect a Republican, 44,276 to elect a Populist, and only 21,078 to elect a Democrat.

To come nearer home, did not Mr. Reid return to power at the 1898 election in New South Wales although the Opposition polled a majority of 15,000 against him? The last election in Victoria illustrates nothing so much as the chaotic state of parties, brought about by newspaper influence in promoting false lines of division. No less than 30 seats, representing 81,857 votes, were contested only by candidates who professed to be Ministerialists of various shades. Of 52 seats contested by Ministerial and Opposition candidates, each party secured 26; but the Ministerialists paid 59,255 votes for their seats as against 44,327 cast for the Opposition. 13 seats were uncontested, 9 Ministerial and 4 Opposition, giving a total of 65 members to the Ministerial party and 30 members to the Opposition.

The arbitrary and haphazard character of these results is obvious. It would be entirely removed by the reform. Every election would reflect the true feeling of the country; the right of the majority to rule would be rendered certain, and the right of the minority to a fair hearing would be assured. Taking the country as a whole, the Ministerialists would pay almost exactly the same number of votes for each seat as the Opposition. In each separate electorate the accuracy would not be so great, but the rectification of even this slight and unavoidable inequality would, instead of being arbitrary, be subject to the laws of chance.

Ineffective Votes.—Under the present system, all votes cast for rejected candidates are ineffective; therefore nearly one-half of the electors have no voice in the Government. A Liberal elector may live in a Conservative constituency all his life without having the opportunity to cast an effective vote. The evil of popular indifference is largely to be explained by this fact. It is no answer to say that it affects both parties equally. The trouble is that nearly one-half of the electors of each party have no influence in deciding who are to represent the party, and therefore do not help to frame its policy.

This evil would also be entirely removed. Every vote cast would count to one or the other party. It is not necessary that every vote should be counted to some one candidate, as the advocates of the Hare system claim. Votes given to rejected candidates would be in effect just as much transferred to the successful candidates as by the Hare system. Moreover, it is an important gain that the candidates of each party would be ranged in order of favour, as the relative position of the candidates would be an index of the feeling of each electorate, not only as regards men but also as regards measures. Therefore, even the votes given to rejected candidates would affect the framing of the party policy, and show the progress of public opinion.

Uncontested Seats.—At the 1895 election for the Imperial Parliament no less than 189 seats out of 670 were uncontested. Thus one-quarter of the people had no opportunity of expressing any opinion. In Australia the proportion is often quite as large. The present Legislative Council of Victoria is an extreme instance. One-third of the Council retires every three years; and at the last election not a single seat was contested. Only 4 out of the 48 sitting members have had to contest election. Under these circumstances the holding of an election at all becomes a farce. No doubt it is very convenient for the favoured individuals; but as the primary object of elections is the ascertainment of public opinion, it is very desirable that every seat should be contested.

The chief cause of this evil is that when one party is strong in an electorate it is hopeless for the minority to contest it, unless the majority nominates more than one candidate. On the other hand, the majority knows that if it does split its votes the minority will probably win the seat. The result is that the sitting member has a great advantage, and is often tolerated even though he is acceptable to only a minority of his own party.

With the reform each electorate would become the scene of a contest between the two parties for their proportional share of representation. It is very unlikely, indeed, that in any electorate no more candidates would be nominated than are required to be elected.

Limitation of Choice.—Even when seats are contested, the elector's choice is very limited under the present system. Wherever party government is strong, each party nominates only one candidate, owing to the danger of splitting up its votes and so losing the seat. The elector has then practically no choice. He may disapprove of the candidate standing for his own party, but the only alternative is to stultify himself by supporting the opposing candidate. If in disgust he abstains from voting altogether, it is the same as giving each candidate half his vote. Even when two or three candidates of his own party are nominated, and he supports the one whose views coincide most closely with his own, he can exert very little direct influence on the party policy. Besides, he will often think it wise to support the strongest candidate rather than the one he favours most.

These considerations show what a very imperfect instrument the present system is for expressing public opinion. The test which should be applied to any system of election is whether it allows each elector to express his opinion on general policy, and from this point of view the present system fails lamentably; all opinion which does not run in the direct channel of party is excluded. Mr. Bryce has fixed on this defect as the weak point of the party system, but the fault really lies in the limitation of choice connected with the present system of election. It is quite true that "in every country voting for a man is an inadequate way of expressing one's views of policy, because the candidate is sure to differ in one or more questions from many of those who belong to the party."[4] But if, in the first place, the incentive to limit the number of candidates be removed and the field of choice widened, and if, in the second place, each elector be allowed to vote for several candidates instead of one only, the defect would be remedied. Now, the reform makes both these provisions, and the importance of the improvement can hardly be overrated. It means, first, that every elector will be not only allowed, but also induced, to express his opinion on general policy. He may give his votes to candidates either for their general views or for some particular view; or, if he lays less stress on measures than on men, he may give them to men of high character or of great administrative ability. It means, secondly, that every section of opinion composing each party will be fairly represented, and that none will be excluded, because the candidates of each party will compete among themselves for the support of all sections, in order to decide those most in general favour. Hence every section will directly help to frame and influence the party policy, and there will be not the slightest excuse for independent action outside the two main parties. In the third place, it means the substitution of individual responsibility for the corporate responsibility of parties, since the electors will have the power to reject those who wish to modify party action in any direction contrary to the general wish. It means, finally, that every elector's opinion, as expressed by his vote, will have equal influence in deciding the direction of party action.

Control of Nominations.—There is a constant incentive with the present system of election to limit the number of candidates to two, one representing each party. For if either party splits up its votes on more than one candidate it will risk losing the seat. But the necessity to limit the candidates involves some control of the nominations, and this is perhaps the worst feature of the system. It means that, instead of the electors being allowed to select their representative, he is chosen for them by some irresponsible body. We have seen how in the United States the nominating system is the source of the power of the "boss" and the "machine;" and the same result is only a matter of time in British countries. The registration of voters is not yet conducted in the same rigid manner as in America, nor is the farce of holding a primary election gone through; but whether the control be exercised by a political organization, a newspaper, a local committee, or a secret society, the principle is the same. Mr. Bryce has noticed the rapid change in the practice of England on this point:—"As late as the general elections of 1868 and 1874 nearly all candidates offered themselves to the constituency, though some professed to do so in pursuance of requisitions emanating from the electors. In 1880 many—I think most—Liberal candidates in boroughs and some in counties were chosen by the local party associations, and appealed to the Liberal electors on the ground of having been so chosen. In 1885, and again in 1892, all, or nearly all, new Liberal candidates were so chosen, and a man offering himself against the nominee of the association was denounced as an interloper and traitor to the party. The same process has been going on in the Tory party, though more slowly. The influence of the locally wealthy, and also that of the central party office, is somewhat greater among the Tories, but in course of time choice by representative associations will doubtless become the rule."[5] Is it to be expected that this power will not be abused as in America? The trouble is that no association can represent all the party electors, and that the representative becomes responsible to the managers of the association, to whom he really owes his election. Any control of this kind is fatal to the principle of responsible leadership. And yet the only alternative with the present method of election is the break-up of the party system. This is the dilemma in which all modern democracies are placed. The evil will be completely obviated by the reform. Instead of limiting the candidates, it will be to the advantage of each party to induce the strongest and most popular candidates to stand on its behalf, since the number of seats it will obtain depends only on the aggregate votes polled by all the candidates. With individual candidature there can be no "machine" control of nominations. All are free to appeal directly to the people.

Localization of Politics.—The local delegate is unfortunately the prevailing type of Australian politician. The value of a member is too often measured by the services he renders to his constituents individually or the amount of money he can get the Government to spend in his constituency. Hence the nefarious practice of log-rolling in Parliament. Is it any wonder that some of the colonies promise to rival France in the proportion of unreproductive works constructed out of loan money?

How few of our members approach the ideal expressed by Edmund Burke in his address to the electors of Bristol:—"Parliament is not a congress of ambassadors from different and hostile interests, which interests each must maintain, as an agent and advocate, against other agents and advocates; but Parliament is a deliberative assembly of our nation, with one interest—that of the whole—where not local purposes, not local prejudices, ought to guide, but the general good, resulting from the general reason of the whole. You choose a member, indeed, but when you have chosen him he is not a member of Bristol, but he is a member of Parliament." It must be confessed, however, that Burke's ideal is rather exalted; it is the duty of a member to make known the requirements of his district. It is the ministry which is specially charged with looking after the interest of the whole and of resisting illegitimate demands. But it cannot do so if its position is so insecure that it must purchase the support of the "parish pump" politician.

The only way to nationalize politics is to ensure that every electorate shall be contested on national issues by organized parties, and that every locality shall be represented on both parties. The proposed system will provide this remedy. In enlarged electorates each party will take good care that its candidates are men of local influence in the most important divisions of the electorate; therefore, sectional and local interests will be represented, but they will be subordinated to the interests of the whole electorate; and where there are a few large divisions the interests of each will more nearly coincide with national interests than where there are a large number of small divisions. Besides, log-rolling will not be so easy between groups of representatives as among single representatives.

Incentive to Bribery and Corruption.—We now come to a class of evils which to a large extent result from the fact that a few votes in each electorate decide whether a party gets all the representation or none at all. Candidates are impelled, in order to gain support from every faction, to acts degrading to themselves and destructive to the moral tone of the people. Foremost among these evils is the great incentive to bribery and corruption; it is manifested not only in direct expenditure at the elections, but also in promises of patronage and class advantages. Direct bribery is perhaps worst in America; Professor M. Cook states, in a paper on "The Alarming Proportion of Venal Voters" in the Forum for September, 1892, that in twenty-one towns of Connecticut 16 per cent, of the voters are venal. As Professor Commons remarks:—"It is plain that the bribable voters themselves are adequate to hold the balance of power between the parties. The single-membered district, therefore, places a magnificent premium upon bribery." In England the Corrupt Practices Act has done immense good: nothing reflects so much honour on the Imperial Parliament as the voluntary transference of the duty of deciding cases to the judiciary. In Australia this much-needed reform has not yet been introduced, and direct bribery prevails to a much larger extent than would be supposed from the number of cases investigated. Members of Parliament are naturally loth to convict one of their own number, and the knowledge of this fact prevents petitions being lodged.

The mere existence of secret bribery is bad enough, but a greater danger is that acts of indirect bribery are openly practised, with the tacit approval of electors. "There have been instances," says Mr. Lecky, in his "Democracy and Liberty," "in which the political votes of the police force, of the P.O. officials, of the civil service clerks have been avowedly marshalled for the purpose of obtaining particular class advantages—a disintegrated majority is strongly tempted to conciliate every detached group of votes." In Australia this has become a regular practice; and a still worse feature is that Members of Parliament have free access to public departments to promote class and local interests. Class legislation is frequently brought forward on the eve of an election with the sole object of influencing votes. These conditions favour the wire-pullers and mere self-seekers, and, in so far as they prevent the electors from voting on the political views and personal merits of the candidates, they are inimical to the public interests. Mr. Lecky has pointed out that a certain amount of moral compromise is necessary in public life, and that a politician may indulge in popularity-hunting from honourable public motives; the danger is that unworthy politicians may screen themselves under shelter of this excuse.

We do not claim that the proposed system would abolish corruption, but we are justified in hoping that it would mitigate it very much. Even if the venal vote still held the balance of power between parties, parties are not so easily corrupted as individuals. But the most important gain is that it could only exert an influence proportional to its numbers; it could not decide whether a party gets all the representation or none at all, as at present. In most cases it would be doubtful if it would affect a single candidate. Consider, again, the case of individual candidates of the same party; any candidate resorting to bribery in order to increase his chance of election would do so partly at the expense of the other candidates of his own party, who would immediately denounce him. Instead of being forced to conciliate selfish factions, the candidates would be free to appeal for the support of the unselfish sections.

Continual Change in Electoral Boundaries.—The irregular growth of population necessitates a periodical revision of the electoral boundaries of single-membered electorates. Owing to the influence of vested interests, this is generally effected in an arbitrary manner; and the glaring anomalies only are rectified. We have in Victoria at the present day some country electorates with 6,000 electors on the rolls and others with only 1,500. An elector in the latter has four times the voting power of an elector in the former. The process of alteration of the boundaries offers great temptation to unfairness; and in American politics the opportunity is taken full advantage of by a practice which has received the name of the gerrymander. In his work on "Proportional Representation" Professor Commons writes:—

It is difficult to express the opprobrium rightly belonging to so iniquitous a practice as the gerrymander; but its enormity is not appreciated, just as brutal prize-fighting is not reprobated providing it be fought according to the rules. Both political parties practise it, and neither can condemn the other. They simply do what is natural: make the most of their opportunities as far as permitted by the constitution and system under which both are working. The gerrymander is not produced by the iniquity of parties, it is the outcome of the district system. If representatives are elected in this way there must be some public authority for outlining the districts. And who shall be the judge to say where the line shall be drawn? Exact equality is impossible, and who shall set the limit beyond which inequality shall not be pressed? Every apportionment act that has been passed in this or any other country has involved inequality; and it would be absurd to ask a political party to pass such an act and give the advantage of the inequality to the opposite party. Consequently, every apportionment act involves more or less of the gerrymander. The gerrymander is simply such a thoughtful construction of districts as will economize the votes of the party in power by giving it small majorities in a large number of districts, and coop up the opposing party with overwhelming majorities in a large number of districts. This may involve a very distortionate and uncomely "scientific" boundary, and the joining together of distant and unrelated localities into a single district; such was the case in the famous original act of Governor Gerry, of Massachusetts, whence the practice obtained its amphibian name.[6] But it is not always necessary that districts be cut into distortionate shapes in order to accomplish these unjust results. (pp. 49, 50.)

He illustrates a gerrymander which actually made one Democratic vote equal to five Republican votes. We have quoted this description of the methods of the gerrymander not so much because the evil has attained any magnitude in Australia as because it offers a warning of the probable result of adopting the single-membered district system for our Federal legislature.

With enlarged or grouped electorates the periodical revision of boundaries would be entirely obviated, because the size of the electorate may be kept constant, and the number of representatives varied. Under such a system all unfairness would disappear, and the gerrymander would be impossible. Representation would automatically follow the movements of population.

FOOTNOTES:
[4] Bryce, "The American Commonwealth," vol ii, p 325
[5] Bryce, "The American Commonwealth," vol. ii., note on p. 81.
[6] Governor Gerry contrived an electorate which resembled a salamander in shape.

THE HARE SYSTEM OF PROPORTIONAL DELEGATION

The single transferable vote, generally known as the Hare system, was first invented by a Danish statesman, M. Andrae, and was used for the election of a portion of the "Rigsraad" in 1855. In 1857 Mr. Thomas Hare, barrister-at-law, published it independently in England in a pamphlet on "The Machinery of Representation." This formed the basis of the scheme elaborated in his "Election of Representatives," which appeared in 1859.

He proposed to abolish all geographical boundaries by constituting the whole of the United Kingdom one electorate for the return of the 654 members of the House of Commons. Each member was to be elected by an equal unanimous number of electors. The method of election was therefore so contrived as to allow the electors to group themselves into 654 constituencies, each group bound only by the tie of voluntary association, and gathered from every corner of the Kingdom. The total number of votes cast (about a million) was to be divided by 654, and the quotient, say about 1,500, would be the quota or number of votes required to elect a member. But some of the candidates would naturally receive more votes than the quota, and a great many more would receive less. How were all the votes to be equally divided among 654 members so that each should secure exactly the quota? The single transferable vote was proposed to attain this result. Each elector's vote was to count for one candidate only, but he was allowed to say in advance to whom he would wish his vote transferred in case it could not be used for his first choice. Each ballot paper was, therefore, to contain the names of a number of candidates in order of preference—1, 2, 3, andc. Then all the candidates having more than a quota of first choices were to have the surplus votes taken from them and transferred to the second choice on the papers, or if the second choice already had enough votes, to the third choice, and so on. When all the surpluses were distributed a certain number of members would be declared elected, each with a quota of votes. The candidates who had received the least amount of support were then to be gradually eliminated. The lowest candidate would be first rejected, and his votes transferred to the next available preference on his ballot papers; then the next lowest would be rejected, and so on till all the votes were equally distributed among the 654 members. Such was the Hare system as propounded by its author. The electors were to divide themselves into voluntary groups; then the groups which were too large were to be cut down by transferring the surplus votes, and the smaller groups were to be excluded and the votes also transferred until the groups were reduced to 654 equal constituencies. These two processes, transferring surplus votes and transferring votes from excluded candidates, are the main features of the system. Mr. Hare's rules for carrying them out are drawn up in the form of a proposed electoral law, and in the different editions of his work the clauses vary somewhat. They are also complicated by an impossible attempt to retain the local nomenclature of members. As regards surplus votes it was provided that the ballot papers which had the most preferences expressed should be transferred; still a good deal was left to chance or to the sweet will of the returning officer, and this has always been admitted as a serious objection. The process of elimination is still more unsatisfactory. Mr. Hare was from the first strongly opposed to the elimination of the candidate who had least first preferences, and he therefore proposed that, in order to decide which candidate had least support, all expressed preferences should be counted. This involved such enormous complication that in the 1861 edition of his work he abandoned the process of elimination altogether in favour of a process of selection. He then proposed to distribute surplus votes only, and to elect the highest of the remainder, regardless of the fact that they had less than a quota. He then wrote:—"The reduction of the number of candidates remaining at this stage of the election may be effected by taking out the names of all those who have the smallest number of actual votes—that is, who are named at the head of the smallest number of voting papers, and appropriating each vote to the candidate standing next in order on each paper. This process would be so arbitrary and inequitable in its operation as to be intolerable. It might have the effect of cancelling step by step more votes given to one candidate than would be sufficient to return another.... Such a process disregards the legitimate rights both of electors and of candidates." But the process of selection was not proportional representation at all, being practically equivalent to a single untransferable vote, and Mr. Hare finally adopted, in spite of its defects, the "arbitrary and inequitable" process of elimination in his last edition in 1873. And all his recent disciples have been forced to do the same, because nothing better is known.

Mr. Hare's scheme has ceased to be of any practical interest, since it is now generally admitted that electorates should not return more than ten or twenty members. Moreover, it is admitted that the electors would group themselves in very undesirable ways, and not as Mr. Hare expected. And yet the only effect of limiting the size of the electorates is to reduce the number of undesirable ways in which electors might group themselves. Let us briefly note the different proposals which have been made.

1. Sir John Lubbock's Method.—In his work on "Representation," Sir John Lubbock says:—"The full advantage of the single transferable vote would require a system of large constituencies returning three or five members each, thus securing a true representation of opinion." Three-seat electorates are, however, too small to secure accurate proportional representation; with parties evenly balanced, for instance, one must secure twice as much representation as the other.

The following rules are given to explain the working of the system:—

(1) Each voter shall have one vote, but may vote in the alternative for as many of the candidates as he pleases by writing the figures 1, 2, 3, etc, opposite the names of those candidates in the order of his preference.

COUNTING VOTES.

(2) The ballot papers, having been all mixed, shall be drawn out in succession and stamped with numbers so that no two shall bear the same number.

(3) The number obtained by dividing the whole number of good ballot papers tendered at the election by the number of members to be elected plus one, and increasing the quotient (or where it is fractional the integral part of the quotient) by one, shall be called the quota.

(4) Every candidate who has a number of first votes equal to or greater than the quota shall be declared elected, and so many of the ballot papers containing those votes as shall be equal in number to the quota (being those stamped with the lowest numerals) shall be set aside as of no further use. On all ballot papers the name of the elected candidate shall be deemed to be cancelled, with the effect of raising by so much in the order of preference all votes given to other candidates after him. This process shall be repeated until no candidate has more than a quota of first votes or votes deemed first.

(5) Then the candidate or candidates having the fewest first votes, or votes deemed first, shall be declared not to be elected, with the effect of raising by so much in the order of preference all votes given to candidates after him or them, and rule 4 shall be again applied if possible.

(6) When by successive applications of rules 4 and 5 the number of candidates is reduced to the number of members remaining to be elected, the remaining candidates shall be declared elected.

Objection is commonly taken to this method on account of the element of chance involved in the distribution of surplus votes. Suppose the quota to be 1,000, and a candidate to receive 1,100 votes, the 100 votes to be transferred would be those stamped with the highest numerals. But if the hundred stamped with the lowest numerals or any other hundred had been taken the second choices would be different.

Strictly speaking, however, this is not a chance selection—it is an arbitrary selection. The returning officer must transfer certain definite papers; if he were allowed to make a chance selection it would be in his power to favour some of the candidates.

Sir John Lubbock points out that the element of chance might be eliminated by distributing the second votes proportionally to the second choices on the whole 1,100 papers, and that it might be desirable to leave any candidate the right to claim that this should be done if he thought it worth while.

2.—The Hare-Clark Method.—The Hare system has been in actual use in Tasmania for the last two elections. It is applied only in a six-seat electorate at Hobart and a four-seat electorate at Launceston. The rules for distributing surplus votes proportionally were drawn up by Mr. A.I. Clark, late Attorney-General. The problem is not so simple as it appears at first sight. There is no difficulty with a surplus on the first count; it is when surpluses are created in subsequent counts by transferred votes that the conditions become complicated. Mr. Clark adopts a rule that in the latter case the transferred papers only are to be taken into account in deciding the proportional distribution of the surplus. Suppose, as before, the quota to be 1,000 votes, and a candidate to have 1,100 votes, 550 of which are marked in the second place to one of the other candidates. Then the latter is entitled to 50 of the surplus votes, and a chance selection is made of the 550 papers. The element of chance still remains, therefore, if this surplus contributes to a fresh surplus.

3.—The Droop-Gregory Method.—This method, advocated by Professor Nanson, of the Melbourne University, is claimed to entirely eliminate the element of chance. The Gregory plan of transferring surplus votes is defined as a fractional method. If a candidate needs only nine-tenths of his votes to make up his quota, instead of distributing the surplus of one-tenth of the papers all the papers are distributed with one-tenth of their value. Reverting to our former example, if a candidate is marked second on 550 out of 1,100 votes, the quota being 1,000 and the surplus 100, then instead of selecting 50 out of the 550 papers, the whole of them would be transferred in a packet, the value of the packet being 50 votes, or, as Professor Nanson prefers to put it, the value of each paper in the packet being one-eleventh of a vote. Should this packet contribute to a new surplus the third choices on the whole of the papers are available as a basis for the redistribution. The packet would be divided into smaller packets, and each assigned its reduced value. It might here be pointed out that the use of fractions is quite unnecessary, the value of each packet in votes being all that is required, and that the-same process may be used with the Hare-Clark method to avoid the chance selection of papers. The only real difference is this: that when a surplus is created by transferred votes Mr. Clark distributes it by reference to the next preference on all the transferred papers, and Professor Nanson by reference to the last packet of transferred papers only—the packet which raises the candidate above the quota.

Which of these methods is correct? Should we select the surplus from all votes, original and transferred, as Sir John Lubbock proposes; from all transferred votes only, with Mr. Clark; or from the last packet only of transferred votes, with Professor Nanson? Consider a group of electors having somewhat more than a quota of votes at its disposal. If it nominates one candidate only every one of the electors will have a voice in the distribution of the surplus, but if it puts up three candidates, two of whom are excluded and the third elected, Mr. Clark would allow those who supported the two excluded candidates to decide the distribution of the surplus, and Professor Nanson only those who supported the last candidate excluded. Both are clearly wrong, for the only rational view to take is that when a candidate is excluded it is the same as if he had never been nominated and the transferred votes had formed part of the original votes of those to whom they are transferred. Whenever a surplus is created it should therefore be distributed by reference to all votes, original and transferred. As regards these surpluses, Mr. Clark and Professor Nanson have adopted an arbitrary basis, which is no more than Sir John Lubbock has done; and they have therefore eliminated the element of chance only for surpluses on the first count. It may be asked, Why cannot all surpluses be distributed by reference to all the papers, if that is the correct method? The answer is that the complication involved is enormous. Yet this was the plan first advocated by Professor Nanson, who wrote, in reply to a definite inquiry how the Gregory principle was applied:—"I explain by an example. A has 2,000 votes, the quota being 1,000. A then requires only half the value of each vote cast for him. Each paper cast for him is then stamped as having lost one-half of its value, and the whole of A's papers are then transferred with diminished value to the second name (unelected, of course). The same principle applies all through. Whenever anyone has a surplus all the papers are passed to the next man with diminished value." Now, the effect of this extraordinary proposal would be that the whole of the papers would have to be kept in circulation till the last candidate was elected, with diminishing compound fractional values. In a ten-seat electorate a large proportion would pass through several transfers, and would towards the end of the count have such a ridiculously small fractional value that it would take several millions of the ballot-papers to make a single vote! It is no wonder that this method was abandoned when the complications to which it would lead were realized.

A simple method of avoiding this complexity would be to treat transferred surplus papers as if the preferences were exhausted. It must be remembered that in all transfers a certain number of papers are lost owing to the preferences being exhausted, and the additional loss would be small. Thus at the first Hobart election 206 votes were wasted, and this number would have been increased by two only. Every surplus would then be transferred by reference to the next choice, wherever expressed, on both original papers and papers transferred from excluded candidates.

It might be provided, however, for greater accuracy that all papers contributing to surpluses on the first count only should be transferred in packets. Should these contribute to a new surplus, it should be divided into two parts, proportional to (1) original votes and votes transferred from excluded candidates, and (2) the value of the packet in votes. Each part would then be distributed proportionally to the next available preferences wherever expressed. To divide the packets into sub-packets is a useless complication. The loss involved in neglecting them would usually be less than one-thousandth part of the loss due to exhausted papers.

Having now dealt with the main features of the different variations of the Hare system, we may proceed to consider some details which are common to all of them. A difference of opinion exists, however, as regards the quota. Sir John Lubbock and Professor Nanson advocate the Droop quota, which we have shown to be a mathematical error; Miss Spence and Mr. Clark use the correct quota.

The Wrong Candidates are Liable to be Elected.—The Hare system may be criticised from two points of view; first, as applied to the conditions prevailing when it is introduced, and, secondly, as regards the new conditions it would bring about. Its advocates confine themselves to the first point of view, and invariably use illustrations based on the existence of parties.

We readily grant that if the electors vote on party lines, and transfer their votes within the party as assumed, the Hare system would give proportional representation to the parties; but even then it would sacrifice the interests of individual candidates, for it affords no guarantee that the right candidates will be elected. The constant tendency is that favourites of factions within the party will be preferred to general favourites. This at the same time destroys party cohesion, and tends to split up parties. Nor can this result be wondered at, since the very foundation of the system is the separate representation of a number of sections.

One reason why the wrong candidates are liable to be elected is that the electors will not record their honest preferences if the one vote only is effective. They will give their vote to the candidate who is thought to need it most, and the best men will go to the wall because they are thought to be safe. Mr. R.M. Johnston, Government Statistician of Tasmania, confirms this view when he declares—"The aggregate of all counts, whether effective or not, would seem to be the truer index of the general favour in which each candidate stands, because the numbers polled at the first count may be greatly disturbed by the action of those who are interested in the success of two or more favourites who may be pretty well assured of success, but whose order of preference might by some be altered if sudden rumour suggested fears for any one of the favoured group. This accidental action would tend to conceal the true exact measure of favour in the first count." If this statement means anything it is that the three preferences which are required to be expressed should have been all counted as effective votes at the Hobart election instead of one only; and this is exactly what we advocate. It is also admitted that when two candidates ran together at the first Launceston election the more popular candidate was defeated; and again the Argus correspondent writes of the recent Hobart election:—"The defeat of Mr. Nicholls was doubtless due to the fact of his supporters' over-confidence—nothing else explains it. Many people gave him No. 2 votes who would have given him No. 1 votes had they not felt assured of his success."

A second reason why the wrong candidates are liable to be elected is that the process of elimination adopted by all the Hare methods has no mathematical justification. The candidate who is first excluded has one preference only taken account of, while others have many preferences given effect to. We have shown that this glaring injustice was recognized by Mr. Hare, and only adopted as a last resort. Professor Nanson admits that "the process of elimination which has been adopted by all the exponents of Hare's system is not satisfactory," and adds—"I do not know a scientific solution of the difficulty." To bring home the inequity of the process, consider a party which nominates six candidates, A, B, C, D, E, and F, and whose numbers entitle it to three seats, and suppose the electors to vote in the proportions and order shown below on the first count.

FIRST
COUNT.
SECOND
COUNT.
THIRD
COUNT.
FOURTH
COUNT.
7-vote ADEFBC ADEBC AEBC ABC
6-vote EFDACB EDACB EACB ACB

5-vote CEBDFA CEBDA CEBA CBA
4-vote BDFACE BDACE BACE BAC
4-vote DCEFBA DCEBA CEBA CBA
3-vote FBAECD BAECD BAEC BAC

It will be noted that F, having fewest first votes, is eliminated from the second count, D from the third count, and E from the fourth. A has then 13 votes, B 7, and C 9. If the quota be 9 votes, A's surplus would be passed on to B, and A, B, and C would be declared elected. But D, E, and F are the candidates most in general favour, and ought to have been elected. For if any one of the rejected candidates be compared with any one of the successful candidates it will be found that in every case the rejected candidate is higher in order of favour on a majority of the papers. Again, if the Block Vote be applied, by counting three effective votes, the result would be—A 10 votes, B 12, C 9, D 21, E 22, and F 13. D, E, and F would therefore be elected. Thus we see that A, B, and C, the favourites of sections within the party, are elected, and D, E, and F, the candidates most in general favour—those who represent a compromise among the sections—are rejected.

In practice, then, the Hare system discourages compromise among parties, and among sections of parties; and therefore tends to obliterate party lines. This has already happened in Tasmania, where all experience goes to show that the Hare system is equivalent to compulsory plumping. In every election the result would have been exactly the same if each elector voted for one candidate only. The theory that it does not matter how many candidates stand for each party, since votes will be transferred within the party, has been completely disproved. Votes are actually transferred almost indiscriminately. The candidates have not been slow to grasp this fact, and at the last election handbills were distributed giving "explicit reasons why the electors should give their No. 1 to Mr. So-and-so, and their No. 2 to any other person they chose."[7] Three out of every four first preferences are found to be effective, but only one out of every five second preferences, and one out of fifty third preferences. The first preferences, therefore, decide the election.

The actual result is that, in the long run, the Hare system is practically the same as the single untransferable vote. The whole of the elaborate machinery for recording preferences and transferring votes might just as well be entirely dispensed with. The "automatic organization" which it was to provide exists only in the calculations of mathematicians.

A Number of Votes are Wasted.—It is claimed for the Hare system that every vote cast is effective, because it counts for some one candidate. But unless every elector places all the candidates in order of preference some votes are wasted because the preferences become exhausted.

When a paper to be transferred has no further available preferences expressed it is lost. In order to reduce this waste, a vote is held to be informal in the six-seat electorate at Hobart unless at least three preferences are given. Notwithstanding this, the number of such votes wasted was 7 per cent, at the first election and 10 per cent, at the second.

The effect of this waste is that some of the candidates are elected with less than the quota. At the last Hobart election only three out of six members were elected on full quotas, and at Launceston only one out of four. The result is to favour small, compact minorities, and to lead sections to scheme to get representation on the lowest possible terms.

The Droop quota, being smaller than the Tasmanian quota, would have the effect of electing more members on full quotas, and it is often recommended on that account. Indeed, Professor Nanson declares:—"In no circumstances is any candidate elected on less than a quota of votes. The seats for which a quota has not been obtained are filled one after the other, each by a candidate elected by an absolute majority of the whole of the voters. For the seats to be filled in this way all candidates as yet unelected enter into competition. The matter is settled by a reference to the whole of the voting papers. If any unelected candidate now stands first on an absolute majority of all these papers he is elected. But if not, then the weeding-out process is applied until an absolute majority is obtained. The candidate who gets the absolute majority is elected. Should there be another seat, the same process is repeated. If an absolute majority of the whole of the voters cannot be obtained for any candidate, then the candidate who comes nearest to the absolute majority is elected." It will be seen that Professor Nanson proposes to bring to life again all the eliminated candidates, in order to compete against those who have less than the quota. The proportional principle is then to be entirely abandoned, and the seats practically given to the stronger party, although the minority may be clearly entitled to them. The vaunted "one vote one value" is also to be violated, because those who supported the elected candidates are to have an equal voice with those still unrepresented. And finally, the evil is not cured, it is only aggravated, if an eliminated candidate is elected.

The Hare System is not Preferential.—The idea is sedulously fostered that the Hare system is a form of preferential voting, and many people are misled thereby. The act of voting is exalted into an end in itself. The most elaborate provisions are now suggested by Professor Nanson to allow the elector to express his opinion only as far as he likes. The simple and practical method in use in Tasmania of requiring each elector to place a definite number of candidates in order of preference is denounced as an infringement of the elector's freedom. Why force him to express preferences where he does not feel any? The Professor has therefore invented "the principle of the bracket." If the elector cannot discriminate between the merits of a number of candidates he may bracket them all equal in order of favour. Indeed, where he does not indicate any preference at all, the names unmarked are deemed equal. Therefore, if he does not wish his vote transferred to any candidate, he must strike out his name. It is pointed out that a ballot paper can thus be used if there is any kind of preference expressed at all, and the risk of informality is reduced to a minimum. All the bracket papers are to be put into a separate parcel, and do not become "definite" till all the candidates bracketed, except one, are either elected or rejected; the vote is then transferred to that candidate. And as bracketed candidates will occur in original papers, surplus papers, and excluded candidates' papers at every stage of the count, the degree of complication in store for the unhappy returning officer can be imagined.

The whole of these intricate provisions are founded on a patent fallacy. Preferences are not expressed in the Hare system, as in true preferential voting, that they may be given effect to in deciding the election, but simply in order to allow the elector to say in advance to whom he would wish his vote transferred if it cannot be used for his first choice. The elector is allowed to express his opinion about a number of candidates, certainly, but after being put to this trouble only one of his preferences is used. And which one is used depends entirely on the vagaries of the system. The principle of the bracket illustrates this fact; if the elector has no preference the system decides for him. If his first choice just receives the quota the other preferences are not even looked at. Again, of all the electors who vote for rejected candidates, those who are fortunate enough to vote for the worst (who are first excluded) have their second or third preferences given effect to, and few of their votes are wasted; but the votes of those who support the best of them (who are last excluded) are either wasted or given to their remote preferences. In Mr. Hare's original scheme, for instance, the votes of the last 50 candidates excluded would have been nearly all wasted, unless some hundreds of preferences were expressed.

Another claim on which great stress is laid is that by the process of transferring votes every vote counts to some one candidate. This means nothing more than that the votes of rejected candidates are transferred to the successful candidates. Where is the necessity for this? So long as each party secures its just share of representation and elects its most favoured candidates, there is no advantage gained by transferring the votes. Miss Spence even declares that "every Senator elected in this way will represent an equal number of votes, and will rightly have equal weight in the House. According to the block system, there is often a wide disparity between the number of votes for the highest and the lowest man elected." Surely the mere fact of transferring votes till they are equally distributed does not make all the successful candidates equally popular! On the contrary, it is very desirable to know which candidates are most in favour with each party. Ballot Papers Must be Brought Together for Counting.—This is a practical objection to the Hare system, which puts it out of court for large electorates. If the whole of Victoria were constituted one electorate, as at the Federal Convention election, the transference of votes could not be commenced till all the ballot papers had come in from the remote parts of the colony, two or three weeks after the election. On this point Professor Nanson writes:—"In an actual election in Victoria this 'first state of the poll' could be arrived at with the same rapidity as was the result of the recent poll on the Commonwealth Bill. In both cases but one fact is to be gleaned from each voting paper. The results from all parts of the colony would be posted in Collins-street on election day. These results would show exactly how the cat was going to jump. The final results as regards parties would be obvious to all observers, although the result as regards individual candidates would be far from clear. But this, although of vast importance to the candidates themselves, would be a matter of small concern to the great mass of the people." These remarks are based on the assumption that the electors vote on strictly party lines, which a reference to Tasmanian returns will show is not usually the case. Few will be disposed to agree that a knowledge of the successful candidates is a matter of small moment.

FOOTNOTE:
[7] Hobart Mercury

FREE LIST SYSTEM OF PROPORTIONAL DELEGATION

The Liste Libre, or Free List system, is a far simpler and more practical method of proportional representation than the Hare system. The distinctive feature is that it applies the proportional principle not to individual candidates but to parties. But, like the Hare system, it places no restriction on the number of parties. It is therefore particularly adapted to the circumstances of the countries on the Continent of Europe, which, having already a number of strong party organizations, wish to retain them and to do justice to each. Accordingly we find that nearly all experiments in proportional representation to the present time have been confined to those countries.

Perhaps the very earliest attempt to apply the proportional principle was that of Mr. Thomas Gilpin, in a pamphlet, "On the Representation of Minorities of Electors to act with the Majority in Elected Assemblies," published at Philadelphia in 1844. He proposed that electorates should be enlarged, and that each party should nominate a list of candidates equal to the number required to be elected, and should place them in order of preference. Each elector could then vote for one of these lists; and each party would be allotted a number of representatives proportional to the amount of support it received. The highest on each list, to the number allotted, would be elected. It will be seen that this is really a system of double election; for the order of favour of the candidates of any party would have to be decided before the nominations were made.

Only two years afterwards M. Victor Considerant published a similar scheme at Geneva, Switzerland. Each elector was to vote first for a party and then for any number of candidates on the party list whom he preferred.

The party votes were to decide the number of members allotted to each list, and the individual votes the successful candidates.

The little republic of Switzerland has been the scene of nearly all subsequent improvement. In 1867 Professor Ernest Naville founded the Association Réformiste at Geneva to advocate the principle of proportional representation. In 1871 the Association adopted the Liste Libre system, invented by M. Borely, of Nimes, France, in which each elector was to place all the candidates of his party in order of preference. But as this allows the electors little direct influence on their own candidates and none outside of them, a combination of the cumulative vote and the Liste Libre was adopted in 1875. Each elector was to have as many votes as there were seats to be filled, but he could not only give them to any candidates on any list, but he could also give as many votes as he liked to any one candidate. Thus if there were ten seats to be filled the elector could give ten votes to one candidate, or one vote to each of ten candidates, or five votes to one candidate and divide the remaining five among others, and so on. The only condition necessary was that his votes added up to ten. The aggregate votes given to all the candidates of each party were then to be taken as the basis of proportional distribution among the parties and the highest on each list to the number decided were to be elected.

It was not till the year 1890 that this scheme was actually put into practice. The election of 1889 had resulted so unjustly to the Liberal party in the canton of Ticino that an insurrection broke out. This forced the hand of the Federal Government, which had to quell the disturbance, and proportional representation was recommended and adopted. Several other cantons followed suit, and it is expected that the whole of Switzerland will soon adopt the reform.

A modification of this plan has lately been adopted by the Swiss Association. In this later plan electors can give a single vote only to individual candidates, but if they do not use all their votes in this way they may cumulate the balance on any one party list by marking at the head of the list. Thus if the elector in a ten-seat electorate gives five votes to individual candidates, and places a mark at the head of one of the lists, the balance of five votes will count to that list. The aggregate votes given to individual candidates on any list, plus the votes placed at the head of the list, will form the basis of proportional distribution among the lists. This is the plan adopted by the American Proportional Representation League as most nearly suited to American habits, and recommended by Professor Commons in his book on "Proportional Representation."

Belgium has also quite recently adopted a scheme of proportional representation. As in Switzerland, its advent was hastened by political disturbances. The Catholic party, not satisfied with exerting a preponderating influence in the country districts, wished to obtain also its proportionate share of representation in the cities, and proposed a scheme of proportional representation for them only. This caused such ill feeling that riots took place in the streets of Brussels. Finally, proportional representation was promised all round, and became law for both the Chamber of Representatives and the Senate at the latter end of 1899. In Brussels, where there are 18 seats to be filled, a trial election had already been held in 1893 with satisfactory results. Six lists were nominated, the largest being that of the Socialists, who nominated ten candidates; and over 12,000 electors voted. Each elector was allowed 18 votes, and the methods in which he could distribute them were somewhat complicated. He might (1) mark at the head of a list, (2) mark at the head of a list and also opposite one or more candidates on the same list, (3) mark opposite the names of not more than 18 candidates on any list. In the first case his 18 votes counted to the list marked, in the second case one vote was counted to each of the individual candidates marked and the balance counted for the list; in the third case one vote was counted to each candidate marked. The aggregate of votes marked at the head of each list, plus the individual votes on the list, was then taken as the basis of proportional distribution. So many of the votes were cumulated on lists that only about one-fifth of the votes cast were operative in the selection of candidates.

In the bill which has recently become law a new method has therefore been adopted, which gives more power to the party committees, but allows the electors to modify their choice. For this purpose the party organization nominates the candidates in order of preference. The elector may then accept this order by marking at the head of the list, or he may give his vote to any one candidate on the list. If all the electors of a party vote in the first way, those nominated highest on the list, to the number to which the party becomes entitled, are elected. But if all the electors vote in the second way, those with the highest single votes are elected. The actual result will usually be a compromise between the two, and it is evidently the interest of the party organization to place the candidates in their real order of favour, in order that the electors may accept the list. For if an unpopular candidate were placed at the head of the list few would accept it.

The first election under this system has just taken place, and the result was, as expected, to reduce the Clerical representation considerably.

In all the above variations of the Free List system the distribution of seats is effected by dividing the aggregate votes polled by each party by a unit of representation, but three different methods of determining this unit are in use. The first is obtained by simply dividing the total number of votes by the number of seats.

The objection to this unit is that when there are several parties, part of the seats only can be allotted on full units, and the rest have to be allotted to those parties which have the highest remainders or fractions of a unit, and this unduly favours small parties, who do not poll even a single unit. The rule to divide the total votes by the number of seats increased by one, which was first proposed by Mr. H.R. Droop, reduces slightly the number of seats allotted on remainders, and was adopted by the canton of Soluthern in 1895. In Belgium a third plan, devised by Professor D'Hondt, of Brussels, is used, which is designed to prevent any seats being allotted on remainders. This unit is evidently smaller than either of the others, and is to be found by trial. It is only necessary that the sum of the quotients obtained by dividing it into each of the lists shall be equal to the number of seats to be filled.

Suppose a five-seat electorate in which 6,000 votes are divided among four parties, who poll 2,500, 1,850, 900, and 750 votes respectively. Then if we take one-fifth, or 1,200 votes, as the unit, the result would be the following:—

(1) 2,500 = 2 units of representation + 100 remainder = 2 seats.
(2) 1,850 = 1 unit of representation + 650 remainder = 1 seat.
(3) 900 = unit of representation + 900 remainder = 1 seat.
(4) 750 = unit of representation + 750 remainder = 1 seat.

If the Droop unit of one-sixth, or 1,000 votes, be used, the result will be different:—

(1) 2,500 = 2 units of representation + 500 remainder = 2 seats.
(2) 1,850 = 1 unit of representation + 850 remainder = 2 seats.
(3) 900 = unit of representation + 900 remainder = 1 seat.
(4) 750 = unit of representation + 750 remainder = seat.

By the third method any number of votes between 834 and 900 will be found to comply with Professor D'Hondt's condition, and the result would, in this instance, be the same as by the Droop method. Although the highest number was at first used, the lower limit has been adopted in the new bill.

In no case can the proportional distribution be considered satisfactory. If the electorates are small, and the number of parties large, accurate proportional representation is quite out of the question. In Switzerland, however, the electorates are made to contain sometimes as many as 30 seats. The effect of such large electorates must be in time to encourage the formation of a great number of small factions. At the same time there is not so much incentive to split up the parties as by the Hare system.

Passing now to the selection of party candidates, none of the methods can be said to ensure the election of those most in general favour. When electors are allowed to cumulate on individual candidates, the favourites of sections within the party will be elected. If, on the other hand, they are allowed to cumulate on party lists, all votes thus given are ineffective in the selection of the successful candidates. It may be noted that although the nomination of candidates in lists by party organizations is less in accordance with the practice of British countries than the individual candidature of the

Hare system, there is nothing to prevent one candidate being nominated to stand in the place of a party.

A word of warning must be added as to the danger of holding up Belgium and Switzerland as examples of true electoral justice to Australia. The direct government of the people which Switzerland has adopted bears not the slightest resemblance to the representative institutions of British countries. Both the referendum and proportional delegation are suited to direct government and are destructive to party responsible government. The Swiss adopted the referendum to save themselves from the lobbying and plutocratic character of their legislatures. The initiative and proportional delegation have followed because they are complementary reforms. The consequence is that the legislators have been degraded to mere agents for drawing up measures, and leadership has been transferred to the press. It is the peculiar conditions of Switzerland which enable it to tolerate unrestrained majority rule. It is a small country, surrounded by powerful neighbours, whose strength lies in its weakness. Moreover, the people are very conservative. In Zurich, for instance, which is largely devoted to manufactures, a proposal to limit the hours of work in factories to twelve hours a day was rejected by the people. Nor is direct government proving a success; the tyranny of the majority is already apparent. The first federal initiative demanded a measure to prevent the slaughter of animals by bleeding, designed to interfere with the religious rites of the Jews. Despite the fact that it was opposed by the Federal Council, as contrary to the right of religious liberty guaranteed by the Constitution, it was carried by the referendum. Belgium, again, can hardly be taken as a model of constitutional liberty. Surely we in Australia do not want the factious strife of religious, racial, and class sections, which so nearly brought on a revolution last year. Yet this is exactly what proportional delegation to sections would bring about. Belgium has a hard task to reconcile two races so differently constituted as the Walloons and Flemings, and has been able to avoid instability of the ministry so far only because the Clerical party, which is mostly Flemish, still has a majority. The new system has only consecrated the sectional principle, and will do nothing to restore harmony.

PREFERENTIAL VOTING, THE BLOCK VOTE, ETC

Preferential Voting.—Laplace, the great mathematician, to whom we owe so much of the theory of probability, showed more than a century ago that although individual electors may have very different views as to the relative merits of a number of candidates for any office, still the expression of the degree of favour in which the candidates are held by the whole body of electors will be the same if each elector be assumed to have a uniform gradation of preference. Suppose that there are ten candidates, and it is required to place them in order of general favour. Each elector should be required to place the whole ten in the order of his preference, 1, 2, 3, andc. Let the maximum degree of merit be denoted by ten marks, so that every first preference will count as ten marks. Then, although an individual elector might be disposed to give his second preference only five marks, and the rest of his preferences, say, two marks, Laplace demonstrated that it is most probable that the total result would be the same if each elector be assumed to give his second preference nine marks, his third preference eight marks, and so on. Therefore, if all first preferences be multiplied by ten, second preferences by nine, and so on in regular order down to last preferences multiplied by one, the total number of marks will be an index of the order in general favour. If there is one office to be filled, the candidate with the highest number of marks should be elected; if there are two offices, the two highest candidates, and so on.

But the assumed condition must be rigidly complied with; each elector must express his honest preferences. Whether he will do so or not depends upon the circumstances. Laplace recognized this element of human nature, and declared that if electors are swayed by other considerations independent of the merit of the candidates the system would not apply. For instance, if the candidates are the nominees of a number of independent sections, each of which is anxious only to secure the return of its own candidate, and to defeat those who stand most in his way, the tendency will be general to place the more popular candidates, those whose success is most feared, at the bottom of the list, so as to give them as few marks as possible. The result would be to favour mediocre men, or even in extreme cases the most inferior.

Practically, therefore, the system is not applicable where any of the electors are personally interested in the result. If a number of judges were called on to decide the relative merits of several essays or prize designs, and the competitors' names were not known to them, the system might be used. But even in such a case a simpler method is available; for, although it may be difficult to pick out the best, it is generally easy to agree upon the worst. It is usual, then, to gradually eliminate the worst, and when the number is reduced to two to take the decision of the majority.

This process of elimination may be, however, combined with the preferential system, and the result is more accurate than if one count only be made. At the first count the candidate with the fewest marks would be eliminated and his name struck out on all the papers. All those under him on each paper would then go up one point in order of favour, and further counts would be held, eliminating the lowest candidate each time till the candidates were reduced to the number desired. This method is very complicated, and involves a great amount of trouble.

Consider now the case of a voluntary association of individuals, such as a club or society; and suppose that it is required to elect a president or committee. The condition is clearly that he or they should be most in general favour with all the members; and the question whether Preferential Voting is applicable will depend on how united the members are. Now, clubs are not usually, nor should they be, divided into cliques or parties; indeed, if a serious split does take place it generally results in the resignation of part of the club and the formation of a separate organization. But in a live club it is impossible to prevent slight differences of opinion; and an officer-bearer who has the interests of the club at heart must often offend small sections who want to exert undue influence. In an election for president this office-bearer would stand no chance of election if there are several candidates and any small section likes to put him at the bottom of the list, so as to give him as many bad marks as possible. This is the weak point in Preferential Voting; any small section can ensure the rejection of a general favourite. The greater the number of candidates the smaller the minority which is able to do this; dummy candidates may therefore be introduced to make it more certain. The risk would, however, be very much lessened if the process of gradual elimination we have described were adopted.

When we come to the election of representatives to a legislature it is evident at once that Preferential Voting is not applicable at all. We have shown that the true condition required is not the return of candidates most in general favour with both parties, but the return of the candidates most in general favour with each party separately. Preferential Voting would therefore only be applicable if the electors of each party voted separately for its own candidates; and even then it would be open to the objection we have already urged. If it were applied to the two parties voting together the electors would certainly not be influenced only by the merit of the candidates. They might record their honest preferences as regards the candidates of their own party, but they would naturally place the candidates of the opposing party in inverse order of merit. The candidates most in general favour would be those who represented neither party. Suppose there are three candidates for a single seat, two representing large parties of 49 per cent, each, and the third a small party of 2 per cent. The electors of the large parties would be more afraid of one another than of the small party, and would give their second preferences to its candidate. This candidate, representing one-fiftieth of the electors, would then actually be elected; he would receive 202 marks, and neither of the others could possibly secure more than 200. Moreover, he would still be elected if the process of elimination were adopted, since on the second count he would beat either of the other candidates separately by 51 votes to 49.

These plain facts are indisputable. What is to be thought, then, of the claim made by Professor Nanson that Preferential Voting, with the process of elimination, is the most perfect system known for single-membered electorates.

The Block Vote.—The Block Vote, General Ticket, or scrutin de liste, is in general use when there is more than one seat to be filled. Each elector has as many votes as there are members to be elected, and the highest on the list, to the number of representatives required, are successful. Dealing first with elections to a legislative body, the system is eminently unjust to parties. A rigid control of nominations is necessary in the first place, because any party which splits up its votes spoils its chance. Each party will therefore nominate only as many candidates as there are seats, and the stronger of two parties, or the strongest of a number of parties, will elect the entire list. A minority might in the latter case secure all the representation, but the practical effect of the Block Vote is to force the electors to group themselves into two parties only. It therefore has the same beneficial effect as the single electorate of confining representation to the two main parties. This is apparently nob recognized by Professor Nanson, who writes, in his pamphlet on the Hare system:—"Contrast with this the results of the Block system. With strict party voting, which has been assumed throughout, each of the five parties would put forward seven candidates. The seven seats would all be secured by Form, with 44 votes out of a total of 125, and the remaining 81, or more than two-thirds of the voters, would be wholly unrepresented." Does the Professor really think that the 81 (who, by the way, are less than two-thirds) would be so foolish as not to combine and secure all the seats?

The exclusion of the minority in a single-membered electorate excites only a feeling of hopelessness, but when it fails to secure a single representative in an electorate returning several members, a spirit of rankling injustice is aroused. The Block Vote has, therefore, never been tolerated for long in large electorates. In the early history of the United States many of the States adopted it, and sent to Congress a solid delegation of one party or the other. This proved so unjust, and operated so adversely to the federal spirit in promoting combinations of States, that Congress, in 1842, made the single-membered electorate obligatory on all the States.

In France it was adopted at the election for the Chamber of Deputies in 1885. The result as regards parties was about as good as with the single electorate system. The Republicans and Conservative-Monarchists, whose numbers entitled them to 311 and 257 seats respectively, actually secured 366 and 202. But it was abandoned after a trial at this one election.

The Block Vote was adopted in Australia for the election of ten delegates from each colony to the Federal Convention. This was a work in which all parties might fairly have joined together; and in most colonies the people did select the best men, regardless of party. In Victoria, however, the newspapers took on the rôle of the "machine," and the ten candidates nominated by the Age were elected. Many of the supporters of the defeated candidates voted for some on the successful list who just defeated their own favourites. Had this been foreseen they would have thrown away these votes by giving them to those sure to be elected or to those least likely to be elected. The injustice of forcing each elector to vote for the whole ten is thus brought home. We are now threatened with the adoption of the Block Vote for the Federal Senate, and in some of the States for the House of Representatives as well; and it is in the hope of preventing this wrong that the present book is written.

So far we have been considering the Block Vote as applied to the election of a legislature with two or more parties; we now propose to consider it as applied to one party only. It is a matter of common knowledge that the Block Vote, when used for such an election as that of the committee of a club, works very well, and results in the return of the candidates most in general favour with all sections. The reason is, of course, that all sections work together, and members vote for the best men, regardless of sectional lines. We will go further and say that the Block Vote is by far the best method for such purposes, and is superior even to Preferential Voting. In the first place it is free from the defect that a small section can ensure the rejection of a general favourite; and in the second place it rests on at least as secure a theoretical basis. To fix our ideas, suppose there are ten candidates for five members of a committee. Laplace assumed (1) that each member would have a knowledge of the merits of all the ten candidates, (2) that his estimate of the respective candidates would vary arbitrarily between nothing and a maximum degree of merit, (3) that each member would express his honest preferences. The Block Vote, on the other hand, assumes (1) that each member can pick out the five best candidates, and therefore express his opinion as to how the committee should be constituted, (2) that he will be inclined to place these five candidates on one plane of favour and the other five on one plane of non-favour. We submit that the latter assumptions agree more closely with the actual state of affairs. The members can distinguish between candidates who have merit and those who have no merit or of whose merit they are ignorant; to force them, therefore, to place all the candidates in order of preference is to make them express preferences where none exist.[8] On the whole, then, the Block Vote is more likely to place the candidates in their real order of favour.

But some reservation must be made. The Block Vote works best when the number of candidates does not exceed two or three times the number of vacancies. Suppose, first, that the candidates present in the final result a fairly regular order of favour from lowest to highest. Each of the successful candidates will then be supported by at least an absolute majority of the members, providing the number of candidates be not greater than twice the number of vacancies. But if there are four or five times as many candidates as vacancies, none of the successful candidates will have the support of a majority of the members. On the other hand, however, the candidates do not usually present a regular order of favour from lowest to highest when there are a large number of candidates, for there may be a long "tail" of candidates who receive very few votes. The following general rule may therefore be laid down:—The Block Vote works best when the total votes given to rejected candidates do not exceed the total votes given to successful candidates.

The difficulties indicated above were met by the Australian Natives' Association by a plan which provided that no candidate should be elected except by an absolute majority of the voters. The Block Vote is used throughout; and if at the first ballot the required number of candidates do not obtain an absolute majority a second ballot is held, from which those at the bottom of the poll and those who have been elected are eliminated. This process is continued till all the vacancies are filled. Four or five ballots are sometimes required, and the proceedings become very irksome. A sub-committee was recently appointed to investigate the subject, and reported in favour of the Preferential System with one count only. The process of elimination was considered too complicated to be practicable. Now, the conditions presented by these elections, in which a very large number of candidates are generally nominated, are precisely those in which Preferential Voting lends itself most easily to abuse. An insignificant minority may defeat a candidate who should be elected, by placing him at the bottom of their lists.

A variation of the Block Vote may be suggested which is much simpler and better. The preferential ballot papers should be used, and two counts should be made. At the first count the primary half of the preferences should be counted as effective votes, and the candidates should be reduced to twice the number of vacancies. A second count should then be made of the ballot papers, using the Block Vote. All or nearly all the candidates would then obtain an absolute majority, and it is practically impossible that any candidate should be eliminated by the first count who would have had any chance of election in the second.

This plan is far superior to the original method. It is right that members who vote for candidates who are hopelessly out of it should be allowed to transfer their votes; but it is not right that members who first help to elect some candidates at one ballot should have the same voting power as others at subsequent ballots.

The Hare system is sometimes advocated for clubs on account of its supposed just principle. Any live club which adopts it runs the risk of disruption. It merely encourages the formation of cliques and sections; any slight split would be accentuated and rendered permanent.

The Limited Vote.—The injustice of the Block Vote led to the introduction of the Limited Vote, which allows the minority some share of the representation. We have seen that the Block Vote forces each party to try to return all the representation, and of course one party only can succeed. But if neither party be forced to try to return more than it is entitled to each party will get its correct share of representation, providing both parties are equally organized. This leads to the Limited Vote, in which each elector has a number of votes somewhat less than the number of seats.

The Limited Vote was used in England for a number of three-seat electorates, which were created by the Reform Bill of 1867, each elector being allowed to vote for two candidates only. By this means the majority would usually return two candidates and the minority one. Thus the Limited Vote has the same advantage as the Block Vote and the single electorate system, that it tends to confine representation to the two main parties, but it creates an artificial proportion of representation between them. Moreover, it renders strict party organization even more necessary, since each party must arrange to use its voting resources to the best advantage. Consider the three-seat electorate, for instance. The minority will, if it is wise, nominate two candidates only; and the majority may nominate either two or three. But if the majority does divide its votes among three candidates it runs the risk of securing one only. It can do so safely when two conditions are fulfilled: first, it must be sure of polling more than three-fifths of the votes; and, second, it must arrange to distribute all its votes equally among the three candidates. It is not surprising, therefore, to find that the Limited Vote was responsible for introducing "machine" tactics into England. In Birmingham, when Mr. Joseph Chamberlain organized the Liberals and succeeded in carrying all three seats, the electors in each ward were directed how to vote so that as few votes as possible might be wasted. These three-cornered constituencies were abolished by the Redistribution Act of 1884; and Sir John Lubbock, reviewing the experiment, declared—"On the whole, it cannot be denied that under the Limited Vote the views of the electors have been fairly represented."

The system has also been tried to a smaller extent in the United States. In New York 32 of the delegates to a constitutional convention were elected from the State polled as one electorate, each elector being allowed to vote for 16 candidates. Both parties were afraid to split their votes, and the result was that each returned 16. The rest of the delegates were elected in single-membered electorates, and of these the Republicans secured 81 and the Democrats 47. It might here be pointed out that the Republicans might have secured more than 16 of the delegates from the State at large if they had nominated 20 candidates and allowed the laws of chance to regulate their organization. Each elector might have been directed to put the twenty names into his hat, and to reject the first four he pulled out. The same evil is apparent in Boston, where twelve aldermen are elected at large, each elector being allowed seven votes. Each party nominates seven candidates only; and the majority invariably elects seven and the minority five.

The Limited Vote is therefore not a satisfactory solution of the problem of representation. It gives an artificial instead of proportional representation, and it necessitates strict party organization and control of nominations. At the same time it will generally give a very fair representation if parties are not strictly organized, and might well have been adopted for the Federal Convention, five or six votes being allowed instead of ten. Newspaper domination would thus have been prevented.

Election of the Candidate Most in General Favour.—It is often required to ascertain the candidate most in general favour where one party only is concerned, such as an election for leader of the Opposition or president of a club; and the methods in general use are very defective. We do not refer to the theoretical difficulty, which perplexes some persons, of giving effect to the actual degree of favour in which the candidates stand in the electors' minds, but to the simple problem of finding out who is preferred most by the bulk of the electors. Thus it is universally recognised that when two candidates stand the candidate who has the support of an absolute majority of the electors is entitled to election. Yet it is possible that the rejected candidate may be nearly twice as popular. This might happen if the majority held that there was little to choose between the two candidates, while the minority thought they could not be compared. But it is quite evident that such distinctions cannot be recognized; the candidate who is preferred by an absolute majority must be elected. It is when there are more than two candidates that the difficulty arises. To elect the candidate who has most first preferences is open to very serious objection; he may have a small minority of the total votes, and each of the other candidates might be able to beat him single-handed.

The best way to overcome the difficulty is undoubtedly by some process of gradually eliminating the least popular candidates till the number is reduced to two; the candidate with the absolute majority is then elected. We propose to consider the different ways in which elimination might be made. We assume, in the first place, that each elector has cast an advance vote—i.e., that he has placed all the candidates in order of preference. The most primitive method is to eliminate at each successive count the candidate who has least first preferences. This is the method adopted in the Hare system, and we have already shown that it is very defective; in fact, it is no improvement at all. The eliminated candidate might be most in general favour, and might be able to beat each of the other candidates single-handed. A second method is to use Preferential Voting to decide which candidate should be eliminated at each successive count. This is far superior, but it is extremely complicated, and is open to the objection that when there are a large number of candidates a small section may cause the rejection of the general favourite. We propose to describe a method based on the Block Vote which is much simpler, and which does not lend itself to abuse. We have shown that the Block Vote works best when the candidates can be divided into two equal sections of favour and non-favour. Suppose there are four candidates, the first two preferences should therefore be counted as effective votes, instead of the first preference only. The eliminated candidate will then be the least in general favour. A second count is then made of the three candidates left, and the first preferences and half of the second preferences are counted as effective, and the lowest again eliminated. The candidate who has an absolute majority is then elected. The method may be indefinitely extended; if there are five candidates the first two preferences and one-half of the third preferences are counted, and so on. But when there are a great many candidates more than one might be eliminated. Any number up to eight could be safely reduced to four at the first count.

FOOTNOTE:
[8] The bracket principle introduced by Professor Nanson into the Hare system involves a partial recognition of this fact.

ATTEMPTS TO IMPROVE THE PRESENT SYSTEM

The Double Election.—In the preceding chapter we have strongly insisted that the different methods considered for ensuring the return of the candidate acceptable to all sections are not applicable to the election of legislators. The true principles of political representation require, not the election of the candidate most in general favour with both parties, but the election by each party separately of its own most favoured candidates. But as it is impossible for both parties to be represented in a single-membered electorate, the best alternative is that both should contest the seat and one be represented. The present system of election has largely tended to realize this alternative, especially in those countries in which party government was strong, such as England and the United States; and representation has in consequence been confined to the two main parties. In England, where the party system was gradually developed, this result was attained without any rigid control of nominations, because the true party spirit prevailed and personal ambition was subordinated to political principle; and in the United States it was only brought about at the cost of "machine" control of nominations. But on the Continent of Europe, where party government was transplanted from England, it has never really taken root. Each small group nominated its own candidates, and the successful candidate represented only a plurality, and not a majority, of the electors. Instead of a contest between two organized parties there was a scramble among numerous factions.

In France, Belgium, Italy, and Germany an attempt has been made to check this evil by the double election. If at the first election no candidate secures an absolute majority of the votes, a second election is held, for which only the two candidates who head the poll at the first election are allowed to compete. One must then get an absolute majority. The double election has undoubtedly tended to prevent a further splitting up into groups, but the Continental countries offer such poor soil for the growth of party government that it has only restricted the contest to two factions in each electorate; and, of course, the dominant factions are not the same in the various electorates.

The Advance Vote.—In Australia the same evil has become increasingly evident, and it is now no uncommon thing for a candidate to be elected by less than one-third or one-quarter of the total votes. In Queensland a plan has been introduced to meet the evil, under the name of the Advance Vote, which is designed to secure the advantages of the French plan without the trouble and expense of a second election. The electors simply declare in advance at the first election how they would vote at the second election. All that is necessary is that they place the candidates in order of preference, 1, 2, 3, 4, andc. Then, instead of holding a second election between the two who have the greatest number of first preferences, it is merely necessary for the returning officer to consult each ballot paper and see which of these two candidates is higher in order of favour. Thus if one is marked 3 and the other 4, the vote is counted to the candidate marked 3. This device is assumed to give exactly the same result as the French plan, providing only that the same electors vote at both elections, and do not change their views between the two elections.

But in reality it possesses hardly any of the advantages of the French plan. It is another instance of the danger of neglecting the factor of human nature. The French do not go to the trouble and expense of a second election for nothing. Their plan is far the better. First of all, consider the candidates. They know well beforehand that unless one of them gets an absolute majority of the votes at the first election they will be put to the expense and delay of a second election, therefore it is to their interest that the number of candidates be restricted. This tends to keep down the representation to two sections. Next, consider the electors. They know also that unless they give a majority of votes to one of the candidates they will be put to the trouble of voting a second time, therefore they will take good care the votes are not split up, even if the candidates wanted it. What is the result? Simply that in the vast majority of cases one of the candidates gets a majority at the first election, and no second election is necessary; and, most important of all, the tendency to split up is counteracted.

Now take the Queensland system. None of these checks operate. The splitting up into groups is actually encouraged, and it is to the interest of each group to see as many more groups as possible formed, in order to increase its own relative importance, for the delegates of the two strongest groups have a chance of election instead of the strongest group only.

In practice the plan threatens to break down, owing to a practical point being overlooked. It is evident that the success of the Advance Vote depends on the electors marking all the preferences. The ballot paper should be made informal unless all the preferences are given. In Queensland this has not been done, and the consequence is that a large proportion of the electors refuse to give more than one preference. No more conclusive evidence is needed that the scheme has promoted the growth of factions. These electors voluntarily disfranchise themselves rather than vote for any of the other candidates, and of course the very object of the scheme is defeated; the successful candidate cannot secure a majority of the votes cast.

The Exhaustive Ballot.—A bill has just been introduced into the Legislative Assembly of Victoria, providing for a further extension of the principle of the Advance Vote. The plan is favoured by Professor Nanson, and professes to be an improvement on the Queensland plan, although it is only an "instalment of reform" in view of the ultimate adoption of the more perfect Preferential Voting. The Queensland plan is objected to because all but the two highest candidates are thrown out. Suppose, for instance, two candidates stand for the weaker party and three for the stronger party, it is quite likely that all the candidates of the stronger party will be thrown out. Therefore the lowest candidate only of the five should be thrown out. All his papers should be transferred to the candidate who is marked 2 on them; and those below him on all the papers should go up one point in order of favour. If he stood 3 on a paper, the candidate who was 4 would now become 3. Another count of first preferences should then be made, and the lowest again thrown out; and so on till one candidate gets an absolute majority. It is pointed out triumphantly that this plan, which is known as the Exhaustive Ballot, actually saves in this instance all the trouble and expense of no less than three separate elections. The process of elimination is the same as that adopted in the Hare system, and is little, if at all, better than the Queensland plan in securing the election of the right candidate, while as regards the formation of groups it is worse. For this plan actually encourages the groups to split up, since if one candidate nominated by a group is thrown out his vote will be transferred to the others. Therefore the double election is much better than either form of the Advance Vote. They would do nothing towards restoring the one redeeming merit of the single electorate, of confining representation to the two main parties. And all other mathematical schemes founded on the a priori assumption that the candidate most favoured by all sections is entitled to the seat are just as objectionable.

The conclusion that must be reached from all these considerations is that, except when there is a single candidate standing in the interests of each of the two main parties, it is impossible to say with the present system who ought to be elected. The difficulty is one of fundamental principle. The only way to do justice to both parties is to enlarge the electorates so that each can get its proportionate share of representation, and then to provide such machinery as will allow each party separately to elect its most favoured candidates. In no other way can the people be induced to organize into two coherent parties.

APPLICATION OF THE REFORM TO AUSTRALIAN LEGISLATURES

Federal Legislatures.—The keynote of the Australian Federal Constitution, as expressed in the Commonwealth Bill, is full and unreserved trust in the people. This is in direct contrast with the American Constitution, which seeks to place checks on the people by dividing power among the President, the Senate, and the House of Representatives, and assigning to each separate functions. Do we fully realize the dangers as well as the glorious possibilities of unfettered action? Do we sufficiently feel the weight of the responsibility we have undertaken? In reality we have declared to the world the fitness of the Australian democracy to work a Constitution from which the most advanced of the other nations would shrink! We do not hesitate to avow our firm belief that there is only one thing that can save the situation. Unless Australia is to show to the world a warning instead of an example, all her energies must be bent on the formation of two coherent organized parties, dividing each State on national issues, and competing for the support of all classes and all interests in every electorate throughout the Commonwealth.

That is the lesson we have endeavoured to inculcate throughout this book, and we are tempted to quote in support of it the opinion of an American author, Professor Paul S. Reinsch, in a work just published on "World Politics." He says:—

The political experience of the last two centuries has proved that free government and party government are almost convertible terms. It is still as true as when Burke wrote his famous defence of party, in his Thoughts on the Cause of the Present Discontents, that, for the realization of political freedom, the organization of the electorate into regular and permanent parties is necessary. Parliamentary government has attained its highest success only in those countries where political power is held alternately by two great national parties. As soon as factional interests become predominant; as soon as the stability of government depends upon the artificial grouping of minor conflicting interests; as soon as the nation lacks the tonic effect of the mutual criticisms of great organizations, the highest form of free government becomes unattainable. (pp. 327, 328.)

The greatest strain on the Constitution will probably be felt at the outset. Both people and politicians are suddenly called upon to rise to a higher plane of political thought and action. The idea that each State is to send representatives to fight for its own interests must first be got rid of. The only way in which all interests can be reconciled is by each State acting through the national parties. The greatest danger which assails the Commonwealth is the risk of combinations of States dominating party lines; and it is the more imminent that divergent opinions between the larger and the smaller States were already apparent at the Convention. The four smaller States, Western Australia, South Australia, Queensland, and Tasmania, with about one-third of the population, will have two-thirds of the representation in the Senate; while the two large States, Victoria and New South Wales, will have about two-thirds of the representation in the House of Representatives. At the Convention the fear was expressed that the former, representing a majority of the States, and the latter, representing a majority of the people, might come into conflict, and that a deadlock would ensue. It was on this issue that the great struggle at the Convention took place, resulting in the adoption of a double dissolution and a subsequent joint sitting of the two Houses if necessary. By this machinery all disputes will be finally settled. But what will happen if some of the States consider themselves unjustly treated? Even apart from conflicts between the two Houses, if only one State stood aloof from the main parties it could paralyze government, just as Ireland did in the Imperial Parliament. It is evident, then, that the very existence of the Union is bound up in the immediate formation of national parties.

In the United States this lesson was not learned till the Civil War had demonstrated the danger of combinations of States. Since then two great parties have been maintained, even though their existence involves the spoils system and machine organization. In Switzerland, too, the federal tie was not drawn close till after the revolution in 1847, in which the Catholic cantons attempted to secede.

Unfortunately, another cause of dissension menaces the Commonwealth. We allude to the class representation which we have already animadverted upon. The separate representation of sections or classes within the States is just as much to be dreaded as the separate representation of States, and bodes as much ill. It seems not unlikely that the fate of the first Federal ministry will be in the hands of the Labour party, which will be able to dictate its policy. It is utterly inconsistent with the democratic theory that a small minority should have this power; and it is to be hoped that in the wider field of federal politics its true character will be recognized. It is only by the mutual action of two great national parties that the true direction of progress, favoured by the people, can be worked out; a small minority studying only its own interests is sure to be a bad guide. A steady pressure maintained through the two national parties will ensure the recognition of all just demands; such extreme and ill-considered demands as that for the initiative and national referendum can only provoke opposition and cause reaction. Even those who sympathize with the ultimate objects of the Labour unions must see the folly of their present unpatriotic and suicidal tactics.

It is a matter for hope that in the wider sphere of federal politics the irresponsible leadership of the press is not likely to be the power for harm that it is in some of the individual States at present. But while it may not dominate the Federal Parliament as a whole to the same extent, its control over nominations in the States will be quite as great, and immeasurably greater if the Block Vote is adopted. Nor are signs wanting of a union of some of the larger newspaper ventures in the principal States, with a view to increase their power.

Such is a brief review of the outlook. The great requisites essential for progress are the organization of two national parties and responsible leadership in the Federal Parliament. The dangers to the Commonwealth may be summed up under the two heads of lack of organization and irresponsible leadership outside Parliament. Is it possible that the dangers may be avoided and the requisites secured by a change in electoral machinery? Those who have no conception of the working of social forces, and who do not trace the law of causation into the realm of mind, will be inclined to scoff at the suggestion. To them the only hope of improvement lies in appealing to the people to elect better men. They ignore entirely the reciprocal relation of the Parliament and the people, and while recognizing the influence of the people on the character of Parliament, they deny the influence of Parliament on the character of the people. They declare that the people are "free agents" and will have better government when they make up their minds to get it; and no electoral machinery or parliamentary machinery can influence the result. Such is the passive attitude which consciously or unconsciously is almost universally assumed. Yet who can study the history of the British Constitution without being impressed with the fact that every step in the evolution of its machinery was a true sociological invention and had the effect of directing the people's will, which is the motive force, into channels conducive to the general welfare? Take away the responsible leadership of the Cabinet in the British

Parliament, and it would become a sink of corruption like the United States Congress; take away its organization into two national parties, and it would become a rabble like the French Chambers. Now, is not the electoral machinery the connecting link between the people and Parliament, and therefore a vital part in the machinery of government? Does it not actually decide the constitution of Parliament? If this be granted, it follows that unless the electoral machinery be adapted to give effect to these two great principles, parliaments will inevitably decline; and that the present method of election is a very inadequate means of giving effect to them few will deny.

Our claim for the application of the electoral reform set forth in the preceding pages rests simply on the fact that it will give effect to these principles under conditions in which the present system would fail. We press especially for its application to the Federal House of Representatives, which will be the most important Australian representative assembly; for it it there that organization and responsible leadership are most urgently needed. That they will not be obtained if the present schemes of dividing the States into single-membered electorates are adopted is morally certain; and the result can only be disaster and bitter disappointment. If the mathematical devices described in the last chapter are added, the disorganization will be still more complete. And as for the scheme for allowing separate delegation to a number of sections, which is advocated under the name of the Hare system, it would be absolutely fatal. Who can believe that if Mr. Hare's wild scheme to divide the British people into several hundred sections had been adopted 40 years ago the Imperial Parliament would now be an organized assembly?

Take the conditions presented by the first elections for the Federal Parliament, to be held early next year. In some respects it is fortunate that a definite issue is available as a basis of party organization; for there is a general consensus of opinion that all other considerations must be subordinated to a pronouncement on the tariff issue. In an article on "The Liberal Outlook" in United Australia, the Hon. Alfred Deakin writes:—"By the very circumstances of the case the tariff issue cannot but dominate the first election, and determine the fate of the first ministry of the Commonwealth. There will be no time for second thoughts or for suspense of judgment. The first choice of the people will be final on this head. The first Parliament must be either Protectionist or anti-Protectionist, and its first great work an Australian tariff. That is the clear-cut issue. The risk is that a proportion of the representatives may be returned upon other grounds, as the electors as a whole may not realize all that is at stake or make the necessary sacrifices of opinions and preferences to express themselves emphatically on this point." Now, the only way to avoid the risk indicated is to take this one definite issue as the basis of proportional representation. Each State should be divided on it, and should elect its proportional number of Freetrade and Protectionist representatives. Tasmania and Western Australia could conveniently be polled for this purpose each as one electorate; South Australia might be divided into two electorates, Queensland into three, and Victoria and New South Wales into four or five.

It is very desirable that the first election be contested on definite policies advanced by the prospective party leaders; the suggestion that the first ministry should be merely a provisional ministry, to act till the first responsible ministry is formed after the election, is therefore open to serious objection. The leader of the Freetrade party or the leader of the Protectionist party should be chosen as first Federal Premier, and the first election should decide which policy is to be adopted.

Contrast this scheme with the proposals now under consideration. In Victoria, New South Wales, and Queensland bills have been introduced dividing the States into single-membered electorates, and some of the smaller States are inclined to use the Block Vote. In Victoria a bad precedent has been established by giving the party in power the duty of determining boundaries. From time to time it will be necessary to rearrange the boundaries, not only on account of movements of population within the State, but also because the number of representatives which the State is entitled to will vary. Look forward to the time when the State becomes entitled to one more representative; every one of the 23 electorates, in which vested interests will have been created, will have to be altered These are precisely the conditions which have led to the growth of the gerrymander in the United States.

Already the first scheme submitted to the Assembly has been defeated by a combination of country members, who held that Melbourne was allotted a larger share of representation than it now has in the local Parliament. Whatever may be the arguments by which the disparity between the size of town and country electorates be supported in local affairs, surely they cannot apply where national issues only are at stake. The principle of equal electorates is recognized in the Commonwealth Bill by the rules for allotting representation to the States. Why not, then, for the divisions of each State? It is said that a larger proportion of the electors vote in the town, but it is not those only who vote who are represented.

In dividing a State into electorates for the purpose of the reform, the number of electors in each division should therefore form the basis of proportional distribution. The unit of representation would be the total number of electors in the State divided by the number of seats. One representative would be allowed to each division of the State for each unit of representation, and the remaining seats, if any, would go to those divisions with the largest remainders.

Coming now to the Federal Senate, the bill provides that every State, except Queensland, must be polled as one electorate for the election of six senators at the first election and in case of a double dissolution; at intermediate elections three senators only will be elected, as they retire in rotation. This equal representation of the States might be taken to imply that the Senate is intended to represent State rights, and the provision that each State is to be polled as one electorate would seem to support that view. On the other hand, the senators are not required to vote according to States, for it is provided that "each senator shall have one vote;" the vote of a State may therefore be neutralized by its representatives. And again, the Senate is to be elected directly by the people and not by the State legislatures, as at first proposed. To some extent, therefore, the Federal Senate as now constituted presents a new problem in representation, on which it is not advisable to dogmatize. Personal considerations will probably have more weight than in the selection of representatives; but when we reflect that it is really little more than a revising assembly, elected by the same voters as the House of Representatives to deal with the same questions, and having no special functions of its own, the conclusion seems irresistible that the election must be contested by the same national parties, and that the same method of election should be adopted.

Until the Parliament of the Commonwealth prescribes a uniform method of choosing senators, the duty is to be left to the State parliaments; and it is to be regretted that the States have taken no steps to secure uniform action at the first election. In Victoria a fierce newspaper contest is being waged over the Block Vote and the Hare system, and the arguments, being mutually destructive, only go to prove that both are equally objectionable. The Age naturally wishes to have the privilege of electing six senators as it did ten delegates to the Federal Convention, and contends that the majority should elect all the senators; the Argus rushes to the other extreme in declaring that six separate minorities ought to be represented, and ignores the risk that these minorities would be formed on a class or religious basis. The middle position advocated in this book—namely, that majority and minority should each return its proportional share of representation—is free from the objections to both these extreme views.

State Legislatures.—Even after federation the State Houses will still continue to touch at most points the daily lives of the people; they will merely be shorn of some of their powers and drained of some of their best leaders. The fiscal issue, which has had great influence in deciding party lines in the past, will be removed from the arena of strife, leaving no other than an indefinite line of division into Liberals and Conservatives, which in practice tends to become a division into lower and upper classes. This is the danger ahead; and it can only be avoided by the formation of strong party organizations appealing to all classes to work together for the general welfare. Party government is just as necessary in State politics as in national politics.

The present position is intolerable; the disintegration of parties is so complete that there is not a responsible ministry in Australia worthy of the name. Among the causes which have led to this deplorable state of affairs the present method of election is undoubtedly the most potent; it frequently happens that four or five candidates, representing as many groups, contest a single seat. In Victoria, where the state of chaos is perhaps worst, the influence of the press, the existence of a strong Labour section in the Lower House, and the class character of the Upper House, representing property and capital, have been the principal contributing causes.

With the advent of federation a revision of the State constitution is widely demanded, and is likely to be conceded. One of the first steps necessary to restore harmony must be reform of the Upper House by a gradual extension of the franchise and a lowering of the qualification, so as to ensure that elections are freely contested; it is its present unrepresentative character which gives force to the appeals of the radical press and intensifies class divisions.

The relation of State parties to the national parties is an important subject. In the article from which we have already quoted, in United Australia, Mr. Deakin writes:—"There cannot be a series of Liberal parties, one Federal and the others in the States, each going its own way. There must be but one party, with one programme, to which effect will require to be given continuously in both the States and the Commonwealth." He therefore deplores that the Liberal party, together with its "left wing," the Labour class, will be split on the fiscal issue. "It is this apparently unavoidable rupture in the party," he declares, "which endangers its prospects and presents an opportunity to the Conservative classes of either seizing or sharing an authority to which they could not otherwise aspire." If this means that the "Liberal" and Labour classes are entitled by reason of their numbers to a perpetual lease of power in both domains, there can be no more dangerous doctrine. Parties should be decided by questions of progress and financial policy, and not on class lines; and since the State and Federal legislatures have separate spheres of action, parties should be separate also, unless, indeed, they are to be founded on corruption, as in the United States, where the same two parties control not only national and State politics, but city government also.

In the consolidation of public opinion into two definite lines of policy based on the questions to be dealt with lies the only hope, then, of the progress of the individual States within their own range; and in promoting this desirable result the reform advocated in these pages finds its true application.

THOMAS RAMSDEN ASHWORTH

THE CONDITIONS OF SOCIAL PROGRESS

The Agent of Progress.—If the analysis made in the preceding pages of the principles underlying political representation comes to be regarded as correct, the science of sociology must be profoundly affected: for it is a fact that not only the importance but the very existence of the principles involved has been completely missed by speculators in that field. The view we have taken is that representation is the most important sociological invention which has been made in the whole history of the human race; that the successive steps taken in the evolution of the British Constitution mark a series of inventions scarcely less important, and that the resulting institution of party and responsible government is the indispensable agent of democratic progress. We have traced throughout the electoral and parliamentary machinery on which the institution is based the action of two great principles—organization and responsible leadership—and we have shown that these are the mainsprings of the whole mechanism. Yet we find even such an authority as Mr. Herbert Spencer objecting to the party system, on the ground that it lends itself to a one-man or a one-party tyranny.[9] The fact is that it is only when representative government is weak, and approaches direct government, that such a result can happen, and the distinction is so little recognized that a brief recapitulation may be permitted.

The fundamental error is in conceiving representation as merely a means of registering the popular will; many even go so far as to regard it as an imperfect means of ensuring that each single question will be decided according to the will of the majority. All such conceptions really amount to direct government, and where they are given effect to, whether by the referendum or sectional delegation, society is not organized for consistent progress. Indeed, if the lessons of history can be trusted, such a state of society is bound to be wrecked from within by anti-social influences; political power becomes the object of factious strife, and the rule of the majority degenerates into the tyranny of the majority.

We have endeavoured to show that the true conception of representative government involves a recognition of the principles of organization and leadership, and that representation is in consequence a means not only of registering the popular will, but also of organizing and guiding it. In both cases, therefore, the popular will is the ultimate motive force, but in the one case the desires of the people clash, while in the other they are directed into channels conducive to the general welfare. We have regarded it as an essential condition of representative government that the popular will be expressed only as to the direction of progress, that is to say on general policy and not on single questions, and that complete control of progress be then left to the representative body. In no other way can the people be saved from their anti-social tendencies, and induced to express their opinion as to what is best for all. We have seen how the electoral machinery is adapted to organize this expression of the popular will into two alternative directions of progress; how this is effected by the fact of two parties competing for the support of the people on policies expressing these lines of progress; and how the parliamentary machinery allows the stronger of these two parties for the time being complete control of administration and of the direction of progress. The effect of this organization is that the popular will is reduced to effective action in one direction at a time—a result which is not possible with direct government.

Nor is the principle of responsible leadership which is involved in the reciprocal relation of the representative body and the people any less important. Society cannot progress faster than the individual units composing it. True progress lies therefore in raising the standard of public opinion, and it is this principle which ensures that result by reacting upon and moulding individual character. Hence we find that in countries like England, where the principle is operative, progress is effected without supervision and undue interference in the affairs of the individual by the State, while in countries where the principle is not operative, such as the Continental countries of Europe and some of the Australian colonies, the contrary is the case. Legislation should therefore be directed to changing the nature of the individual, and should not be too far in advance of public opinion. This is what Mr. Lester F. Ward, in his work on "Outlines of Sociology," calls attractive legislation. He writes:—

The principle involved in attraction, when applied to social affairs, is simply that of inducing men to act for the good of society. It is that of harmonizing the interests of the individual with those of society, of making it advantageous to the individual to do that which is socially beneficial; not merely in a negative form as an alternative of two evils, as is done when a penalty is attached to an action, but positively, in such a manner that he will exert himself to do those things that society most needs to have done. The sociologist and the statesman should co-operate in discovering the laws of society and the methods of utilizing them, so as to let the social forces flow freely and strongly, untrammelled by penal statutes, mandatory laws, irritating prohibitions, and annoying obstacles. (p. 274.)

Now, we submit that this attractive legislation is possible only when there is no oppressed minority, and is therefore the peculiar province of representative government; for we have shown that the whole machinery is adapted to induce the people to desire only what is best in the interests of society.

Let us briefly examine the bearing of the view that representative machinery is the agent of progress on previous theories of social progress.

Professor Huxley.—No one has more clearly laid down the conditions of social progress than the late Professor Huxley in his essay on Evolution and Ethics. The gradual strengthening of the social bond by the practise of self-restraint in the interests of society he called the ethical process, and he showed that social progress means a checking of the cosmic process at every step and the substitution of this ethical process. This action he compares to that of a gardener in clearing a patch of waste ground. If he relaxes his efforts to maintain the state of art within the garden, weeds will overrun it and the state of nature will return. So the human race is doomed to a constant struggle to maintain the state of art of an organized polity in opposition to the state of nature; to substitute as far as possible social progress for cosmic evolution. He says:—

Let us understand, once for all, that the ethical progress of society depends, not on imitating the cosmic process, still less in running away from it, but in combating it. It may seem an audacious proposal thus to pit the microcosm against the macrocosm, and to set man to subdue nature to his higher ends; but I venture to think that the great intellectual difference between the ancient times with which we have been occupied and our day, lies in the solid foundation we have acquired for the hope that such an enterprise may meet with a certain measure of success....[10]

Moreover, the cosmic nature born with us, and to a large extent necessary for our maintenance, is the outcome of millions of years of severe training, and it would be folly to imagine that a few centuries will suffice to subdue its masterfulness to purely ethical ends. Ethical nature may count upon having to reckon with a tenacious and powerful enemy as long as the world lasts. But, on the other hand, I see no limit to the extent to which intelligence and will, guided by sound principles of investigation, and organized in common effort, may modify the conditions of existence for a period longer than that now covered by history. And much may be done to change the nature of man himself. The intelligence which has converted the brother of the wolf into the faithful guardian of the flock ought to be able to do something towards curbing the instincts of savagery in civilized men.[11]

But Huxley never realized that the real cause of the better prospects of success in modern as contrasted with ancient times is the discovery of representative machinery. "The business," he declared, "of the sovereign authority—which is, or ought to be, simply a delegation of the people appointed to act for its good—appears to me to be not only to enforce the renunciation of the anti-social desires, but wherever it may be necessary to promote the satisfaction of those which are conducive to progress."[12] There is no conception here of the principles of organization and responsible leadership, so necessary in constituting this "delegation."

Herbert Spencer.—By a great many sociologists it is denied that man has his destiny in his own hands, or can by common effort modify the conditions of existence so as to promote progress. The conception which is held to justify this view is that there is an exact correspondence between the progress of human society and the growth of an organism. Foremost among those who take this view is Mr. Herbert Spencer. The close analogy which the progress of the assumed social organism bears to the growth of the physiological organism is worked out in great detail throughout the "Synthetic Philosophy," and is taken to establish "that Biology and Sociology will more or less interpret each other." The practical conclusion which is drawn is that the growth of society must not be interfered with; if the State goes beyond the duty of protection, it becomes an aggressor. So Mr. Spencer is a most uncompromising opponent of State action, even education and public sanitation coming in for his condemnation. Moreover, he holds that if the social organism be let alone it will tend to a future state of society in which social altruism will be so developed that the individual will voluntarily sacrifice himself in the interests of society.

In an essay on The Social Organism ("Essays," Second Series), he writes:—

Strange as the assertion will be thought, our Houses of Parliament discharge in the social economy functions that are, in sundry respects, comparable to those discharged by the cerebral masses in a vertebrate animal.... We may describe the office of the brain as that of averaging the interests of life, physical, intellectual, moral, social; and a good brain is one in which the desires answering to their respective interests are so balanced that the conduct they jointly dictate sacrifices none of them. Similarly we may describe the office of Parliament as that of averaging the interests of the various classes in a community; and a good Parliament is one in which the parties answering to these respective interests are so balanced that their united legislation concedes to each class as much as consists with the claims of the rest.

The error of regarding society merely as an aggregate is here clearly shown, for if the "parties" in Parliament were based on class delegation, as assumed, social progress would be blocked. The only real foundation for the resemblance between society and an organism is this: that unless the individual units composing society reduce themselves to unity of action in a definite direction, society as a whole cannot progress; or, in other words, that the principles of organization and leadership are essential to progress. Yet Mr. Spencer denies that there is any sphere of collective action for the operation of these principles!

Benjamin Kidd.—The "social organism" theory is also the foundation of the theory of social progress with which Mr. Benjamin Kidd startled the scientific world a few years ago in "Social Evolution." While appreciating the importance of the factor of individual reason, he contended that self-restraint by the individual in the interests of society is impossible without an ultra-rational sanction; that, in fact, without this the reason is the most anti-social and anti-evolutionary of all human qualities. The central fact therefore with which we are confronted in our progressive societies is stated as follows:—"The interests of the social organism and those of the individuals comprising it at any particular time are actually antagonistic; they can never be reconciled; they are inherently and essentially irreconcilable." What becomes of this extraordinary proposition if it is clearly established that the amount of reconciliation depends on the extent to which the principles of organization and responsible leadership are given effect to by representative machinery?

Past Progress.—The question will naturally be raised: If a representative body is now the indispensable agent of social progress, how can progress previous to the introduction of representation be explained? The answer is that the same principles were operative, but in different forms, more suited to the stage of social development. Indeed, we may say that, from the time that man emerged from the brute stage and became a social animal, the types of society which have survived in the struggle for existence with the state of nature and with other types have been those in which the principles of organization and leadership have been most active. Even the lowest types of savages, such as the native tribes studied by Professor Baldwin Spencer and Mr. Gillen in Central Australia, have a complicated system of organization, the peculiar feature of which is totemism, or group marriage; but this is more the result of development than of conscious effort. Leadership also is rudimentary, for, although the old men have control of the elaborate ceremonies described, they conform almost entirely to custom and tradition. Out of this savage stage there grew in favoured countries the second type of human society—the patriarchal, in which leadership becomes personal, and centred in a chief who exercises despotic authority. Patriarchal society grew out of the necessities of a pastoral existence; indeed, it was the discovery of the domestication of animals which gave rise to it. Among other interesting features which were developed are permanent marriage, slavery, and ancestor worship. There can be no doubt that the latter played an important part in binding the tribe into one organization, and in inducing all the tribe to submit to the leadership of the chief. There is a second stage of patriarchal society in which the large tribes break up into clans and become less nomadic. Professor Jenks has shown, in his "Short History of Politics," how this stage originated in the adoption of agriculture. We begin now to have the village community, bound by the tie of kinship, and submitting to the leadership of a lord; and are already on the threshold of modern political society, in which all these ancient barriers are broken down and the individual becomes the social unit. The cause of this momentous change is development of the art of warfare. But before we reach the modern State there is an intermediate stage, namely, feudalism. The feudal chief is simply the successful warrior—the leader of a band of adventurers who get control of a definite territory and exact military allegiance from its inhabitants. Out of the consolidation of these bands, or by conquest, modern States were founded. Leadership was now vested in an irresponsible despot—the king; and the trouble was to render this new institution permanent, and to induce the people to submit to it. The former result was attained by making the kingship hereditary, but the latter has always been a difficult task. It is doubtful if it would ever have been accomplished but for a significant alliance—that of Church and State. The convenient fiction of the divine right of kings was invented, and religion was used to bolster up the institution and to provide a sanction for submission to absolutism. In other words, irresponsible leadership was tolerated because responsibility was supposed to exist to a Higher Power. So we find that all the great religious movements—Christianity, Mohammedanism, and even Buddhism—have been associated with the establishment of mighty kingdoms. Moreover, the only two kingdoms in Europe in which absolutism still holds out are Russia and Turkey, in which the head of the State is also head of the Church. But military despotism, which was based solely on the exploitation of weaker communities, of which ancient Rome was the culminating type, wanted the elements of permanent progress, and was bound to disappear before a new type which rested on the development of internal resources. Militarism must therefore be looked on as a real stage of progress; for in contrast with patriarchal society it was competitive, and it broke down many ancient barriers, and prepared the way for industrial co-operation. Thus we arrive at the conditions favourable to the rise of representative institutions. For when the cost of wars had to be raised out of the national resources kings found it convenient to get the consent of the people to taxation. Hence the great movement throughout Western Europe for the establishment of parliaments in the twelfth and thirteenth centuries. Why is it that in

England alone this movement was successful? Partly no doubt because its isolated position was favourable to internal progress, but mainly because it was the only State in which the principles of organization and responsible leadership were continuously given effect to. So it is that in England there was developed that wonderful machinery of representative government which has enabled the people to substitute responsible for irresponsible leadership, and has made the national character what it is. This machinery has now been adopted nearly all over the world, wherever it has been desired to make the popular will felt, but in no case has it sufficed to give effect to the underlying principles to the same extent; and success has been attained only in so far as they have been effective. The lesson of the last century has been that the machinery which proved sufficient in England, where progress was uniform through several centuries, breaks down when the pace of progress is increased. An extreme instance is the recent attempt to introduce party government into Japan, a country just emerging from the feudal stage, an interesting account of which is given in the Nineteenth Century for July, 1899. The experiment failed because the clans could not be divided on questions of political principle. In a greater or less degree that is the fundamental source of difficulty everywhere; if the representative machinery produces only sectional delegation the tendency is back through anarchy to absolutism. Is it not an extraordinary fact, then, that the vital distinction between representation and delegation is so universally ignored? Such is a brief outline of the evolution of human society; however inadequate it may be, it at least serves to illustrate the truth that social progress has never been made in the past except when the principles of organization and leadership have been operative.

Future Progress.—As to the ultimate tendency of future progress it would be pedantry to dogmatize; our task has been the humbler one of pointing out the means by which progress is to be attained. We have assumed, however, that there is a separate sphere of collective action in which government is an instrument for the positive amelioration of social conditions. We are aware that this conclusion is at variance with the two extreme schools of modern thought; on the one hand, with the individualists, who hold that government should only be used for mutual protection and to keep order; and on the other hand, with the socialists, who would leave nothing to individual action. Professor Huxley has reduced the claims of these two schools to absurdity and impossibility respectively; and we believe that the problem of the future is to find out that middle course between the anarchy of the one and the despotism of the other which makes for progress. It seems likely that the state of society we are approaching will be one in which, while natural inequalities will be recognized, neither the artificial inequalities of fanatical individualism nor the artificial equalities of regimental socialism will be tolerated, and every man will enter the rivalry of life on terms of an equality of opportunity. This is the state foreshadowed by Mr. Lester Ward in his "Outlines of Sociology" and called by him Sociocracy. Such ideals, however, serve only to refute false conceptions and offer little practical guidance. What is wanted is a clear recognition of the fact that progress depends on collective effort acting through representative machinery, the efficiency of which depends on the extent to which the principles of organization and responsible leadership are operative. The question with which democratic countries are faced to-day is this: Must it be acknowledged that the people are unfit for self-government, or is the representative machinery defective? We have supported the view that the latter is the case as regards English-speaking-countries at all events; and we have shown that in British countries the remedy lies in improved electoral machinery, while in the United States both electoral and parliamentary machinery are at fault.

FOOTNOTES:

[9] "Principles of Ethics."

[10] "Collected Essays," vol. ix., p. 83.

[11] Ibid., p. 85.

[12] "Collected Essays," vol. i., pp. 275-276.